The Network Society

D0783166

KEY CONCEPTS

The Network Society

Darin Barney

polity

First published in 2004 by Polity Press Ltd.

Polity Press
65 Bridge Street
Cambridge CB2 1UR, UK

Polity Press
350 Main Street
Malden, MA 02148, USA

ISBN: 0-7456-2668-8
ISBN: 0-7456-2669-6 (pb)

A catalogue record for this book is available from the British Library
and has been applied for from the Library of Congress.

Typeset in 10.5 on 12 pt Sabon
by SNP Best-set Typesetter Ltd., Hong Kong
Printed and bound in Great Britain by TJ International Ltd, Padstow, Cornwall

For further information on Polity, visit our website: www.polity.co.uk

Contents

Acknowledgements

I am indebted to several colleagues and friends whose insightful conversation contributed to my understanding of the questions driving this volume. These include Mary Stone, Leslie Shade, Peter Hodgins and Tom Goud. I must also acknowledge the patience and good judgement of the editorial team at Polity Press, especially Andrea Drugan, Ann Bone and Claire Creffield, and the anonymous reviewers of the manuscript, whose suggestions improved its quality immeasurably. Finally, I would like to thank the students who have graced my classrooms at the University of New Brunswick at Saint John, the University of Ottawa and Harvey Mudd College. Their appetite for clarity is responsible for whatever is intelligible in the pages that follow. This book is dedicated to them.

1
Network Society

Like moths to a flame, ambitious minds seek out the spirit of their age. A spirit is a vital or animating principle: in the enchanted vocabulary of the ancient faiths, spirit comports with the soul and is ageless; in the enlightened vocabulary of modern science, the term spirit names a motive force particular in time and place. Thus, the political economist Max Weber, searching in 1904 for the 'spirit of capitalism', employs distinctly modern language in describing spirit as 'an historical individual, i.e. a complex of elements associated in historical reality which we unite into a conceptual whole from the standpoint of their cultural significance' (1958: 47). Weber understood both the religious and the secular dimensions of spirit but, as a social scientist, his aim was to gather the particularities of his historical situation and abstract from these a *concept* that would articulate the principle animating human practices and relationships in that moment. Weber's great insight was his conceptualization of modernity as an 'iron cage' populated by 'specialists without spirit; sensualists without heart' (1958: 182). The spirit of industrial capitalism was, in Weber's estimation, *spiritlessness*: modernity culminates when ascetic devotion to profit as an end in itself recedes into a rather vulgar and progressive technological materialism. The principle animating the modern world is revealed by an eclipse of faith in the possibility of a transcendent animating principle. Paradoxically, the spirit that breathes life into modern industrial society also drives the spirit out of the human soul.

Few moths have come as close to the flame, or captured the spirit of their age so precisely, as Weber did his. Nevertheless, there have been attempts. Presently, one of the more ambitious and intriguing efforts to conceptualize the spirit of the contemporary era is gathered under the phrase 'the network society'. In simple terms, this thesis asserts that the spirit of our age is the spirit of the network: the constitutive principles of networks have become the animating force of individual, social, economic and political life, and this marks the distinction of our period in history. Manuel Castells, the Catalunyan sociologist whose three-volume study of the economy, society and culture of the information age was a singular moment in the articulation of this idea (1996; 1997; 1998), puts the matter as follows: 'as a historical trend, dominant functions and processes are increasingly organized around networks. Networks constitute the new social morphology of our societies, and the diffusion of networking logic substantially modifies the operation and outcomes in processes of production, experience, power and culture' (1996: 469).

The word 'network' describes a structural condition whereby distinct points (often called 'nodes') are related to one another by connections (often called 'ties') that are typically multiple, intersecting and often redundant. A network exists when many nodes (people, firms, computers) are linked to many other nodes, usually by many ties which cross the ties connecting other nodes. Numerous metaphors have been used to describe this type and configuration of relationship – indeed, 'network' itself is one of these – including 'lattice', 'web' and 'matrix', all of which seek to evoke the logic of decentralized, proliferating connectivity which defines the essence of a network. The matrix metaphor is particularly apt in light of what is conceived by the network society thesis. Matrix derives from the Latin *mater* for 'mother' and carries 'womb' as its primary meaning: the possibility is that networks are the womb from which a qualitatively new form of society is being born, a society in which identity, politics and economy are structured, and operate, as networks. This is what is at issue in the idea of the network society, and a critical investigation of this concept, in its various dimensions, is the object of this book.

Later in this chapter, I will return to a closer examination of the nature of the network form, an elaboration of the core elements of the network society thesis, and a brief consideration of how these elements ramify in terms of economics, politics and identity in a holistic account of contemporary society. Before doing this, however, I think it would be helpful to situate the network society thesis in relation to a number of the discourses and theories which have risen to prominence (in some cases, only to fade) in the latter decades of the twentieth century, as theorists have attempted to capture and designate the fluctuating social, political and economic dynamics of this historical juncture.

What is in a name?

The power attached to naming something is considerable. In the Christian account of Creation, God gives to Adam the power to name other creatures, and this constitutes a significant aspect of his dominion over them (Genesis 3:19–20). Thomas Hobbes, in his seventeenth-century masterwork *Leviathan*, asserts that it is names which universalize particulars, and which constitute truth when they are ordered in human affirmations (1968: 102, 105). Thus, to name something is to express dominion over it, to constitute it as true, which are no small powers. Those who attempt to name an age seek to unify or gather its particularities, to establish the truth about it, and to exert some control over its dynamic forces by understanding these to the point of being able to nominate them comprehensively and persuasively. That being said, there is considerable variation amongst these efforts. In some cases, the names assigned to ages are *ideological* insofar as they describe the world as those conferring the name would like it to be in their fondest imaginings. Names such as the Enlightenment, or the Knowledge Society, arguably fall into this category. In other cases, the names seek more objective, disinterested description in the highest tradition of sociology. Sometimes the names result from comprehensive meditation on historical periods that have long since passed; in some cases, those who would name an age apply themselves to the present or, more perilously, to prospecting the future. Finally, various epochal names emphasize variables that differ in kind – some speak to the organization of economic production and relationships (the Industrial Age), some to political activities (the Age of Revolution), others to social structures (the Mass Society).

The period leading to the millennial turn has not suffered from a lack of attempts to name it as an age. James Beniger, in his book *The Control Revolution* (1986), lists no fewer than seventy-five distinct appellations in scholarly and popular circulation between 1950 and 1985, each of which attempted to characterize what were perceived to be definitive and transformative aspects of the period – a flurry of naming which leads one to wonder whether history, in its cunning, will perhaps look back and finally designate ours as the Age of Nomination. The network society thesis is part of this galaxy of recent attempts to capture decisively that of which we are in the midst, and our understanding of it as a discrete concept will benefit from considering the constellation of discourses to which it is related most closely, both conceptually and historically. In this section I would like to focus particular attention on the following discourses of nomination: post-industrialism; information society; post-Fordism; postmodernism; and globalization.

It should be stressed at the outset that each of these phrases, including the 'network society', gathers an array of efforts to articulate the definitive spirit of whatever it is that follows either the realization or the exhaustion of the modern project in the West. In the Western world, modernity has been, among other things, the age of technological industrialism, class divisions, mass societies and markets, conflicting ideologies, and political authority organized at the level of territorial, sovereign nation-states. Whether this period has waned, is in its twilight or has been eclipsed is the subject of profound, but unresolved, intellectual debate and speculation. What is certain is that fluctuations and deviations have been detected in various aspects of this trajectory, and each of these detections has been graced with a name of its own.

Post-industrialism

Industrialism was spawned in the eighteenth century, matured in the nineteenth and culminated in the twentieth. At its core was a set of productive practices which brought with them, and relied upon, a particular range of social arrangements: industrialism was characterized by the mine and factory, the urban city, class divisions and mass consumer markets. Motivated by the appetites of a bourgeois class liberated from the constraints of feudal property relations (in the capitalist model) or the rational egalitarianism of a vanguard elite uncorrupted by self-interest (in the socialist model), and animated by the labour of a working class transformed from a rural peasantry into an urban proletariat, 'industrialism' named the economic face of modernity. The principle of industrialism as an economic model was quite simple: apply human labour (either directly or technologically) to the transformation of basic matter into products which could be circulated and consumed – profitably as marketable commodities in the capitalist model; equitably as centrally distributed collective wealth in the socialist model. Industrialism sought perfection along a number of axes, including the mechanization, rationalization and standardization of production; increased power generation; efficient exploitation of an increasing array of natural resources; and the organization of national mass markets for the consumption of its output (Landes 1969). Industrial production was the engine that generated the enormous economic wealth – inequitably distributed though it may have been in both capitalist and communist societies – which has adorned the modern West.

Theories of post-industrialism attempted to express the transition of industrial economies and societies into what was, at the time, an unknown future. As the 1960s gave way to the 1970s, and the welfare state accelerated its development in many capitalist countries, writers such as Alain Touraine (1971) and Daniel Bell (1973) strove to articulate what they saw as a definitive shift in the industrial paradigm. For these theorists, several crucial dynamics combined to signal a transformation. These included a diversion of the energies of post-industrializing societies away from material manufacturing and towards service provision as their primary economic activity and source of wealth, and a corresponding focus of attention on the exploitation of information and knowledge, as opposed to labour and capital, as crucial economic resources. As Bell wrote, 'A post-industrial society is based on services . . . what counts is not raw muscle power or energy, but information' (1973: 127). This reorientation towards service industries (trade, finance, transport, retailing, health, recreation, research, education, government) was accompanied by the growth of white-collar service occupations relative to blue-collar jobs in industrial manufacturing. Thus, in the post-industrial society, the basis of social and economic stratification would no longer be a property relation turning on ownership of the means of production, but rather control over systemic information and knowledge: a new class of technocrats, managers, professional engineers and scientists would replace the owners of factories and mines at the top of the social and political hierarchy, and those executing the more menial tasks of service delivery would replace the industrial proletariat at its bottom. As we will see, an updated version of this part of the post-industrial thesis is central to accounts of the network society.

Some theorists of post-industrialism, such as Bell, saw in this shift the potential to overcome the more degrading and unjust aspects of the industrial era. Images of the post-industrial future were characteristically infused with heady optimism: post-industrial society, it was imagined, would bring with it a more educated, leisured and engaged citizenry, a levelling of economic inequality, a thriving global economy, scientific advance immune to ideology, and rational management of public affairs. There were, however, others – including Touraine (1971), Herbert Marcuse (1964) and Jacques Ellul (1964) – who saw in post-industrialism the harbinger of a 'programmed' or 'one-dimensional' society which would deepen the alienation of capitalism, in which human life would increasingly be subjected to domination and irrational exploitation masquerading as objectively rational technique. Thus, the differences between industrial and post-industrial society were differences in degree – of the sophistication of domination and the depth of alienation – rather than kind.

Yet another body of opinion challenged the theory of post-industrialism on a more empirical level. In their influential book *Manufacturing Matters*, Stephen Cohen and John Zysman (1987: 261) contended that 'There is no such thing as a post-industrial economy.' In the view of these authors and others (see Woodward 1980), post-industrialism named an ideology, not an economic reality. While it was undeniable that micro-electronics technologies were having considerable effects on production practices, the shift away from manufacturing towards service was, in this view, wildly exaggerated, as were claims regarding a 'revolution' in the basic practices and relationships of industrial capitalism. In short, according to these critics, to the extent a socio-economic shift was occurring, it was not a shift from industry to service or knowledge, but rather simply a transition 'from one kind of industrial society to another' (Cohen and Zysman 1987: 260).

Information society

The fortunes of post-industrialism were dashed upon the energy crisis and ensuing recessions in the Atlantic economies during the 1970s. Around the same time, Japanese scholars and policy-makers were beginning to sketch the contours of a model for society and economy which revolved specifically around the increasingly flexible functionality of microcomputers. The name chosen for this model was *joho shakai*, which translates roughly as 'information society'. In many ways, the information society model represents an echo of the theory of post-industrialism, albeit one with a sharper articulation of the role of computing technology and knowledge in the abstract form of information. As imagined by Japanese futurist Yoneji Masuda (1981) *joho shakai* would replace the production of 'material values' with the mass production and circulation of 'information values'. At the core of the information society would be the computer, the fundamental economic function of which would be to augment and replace mental labour, yielding increased leisure and new information-based industries. In social and political terms, information societies would feature voluntary communities, participatory democracy, generalized affluence, equality and psychic well-being; the information society would be, in Masuda's vision, a 'Computopia' in which a person could 'paint one's own design on the invisible canvas of one's future, and then set out to create it' (Masuda 1981). As we will see in chapter 5, these themes remain significant in discussions of identity in the network society.

By the late 1970s, as the decade's economic downturn continued, intellectuals in Europe and North America were beginning to consider seriously the new Japanese approach to maintaining productivity and growth. In the United States, Marc Porat published a study entitled *The Information Economy* (1977) in which he attempted to define and measure the contours of the information sector – including the nature of its workforce and occupational structure – and its ancillary activities. Porat's findings indicated that, by as early as 1967, 'information activities' accounted for 46 per cent of the United States's gross national product, and 'information workers' comprised 40 per cent of the country's labour pool (Porat 1977: 8). There was certainly debate over the integrity and definition of Porat's categories, but here was persuasive empirical evidence that 1970s America was *already* an Information Society. Notable theorists of post-industrialism such as Daniel Bell (1979) began to rearticulate their analyses in the language of computerization and information. In 1978, Simon Nora and Alain Minc published *L'Informatisation de la Société*, translated as *The Computerization of Society* (1981), a report on computerization for the French government. In it they surmised that the 'increasing interconnections between computers and telecommunications' would 'alter the entire nervous system of social organization . . . open radically new horizons . . . [transform] the pattern of our culture . . . affect the economic balance, modify power relationships, and increase the stakes of sovereignty' (Nora and Minc 1981: 3–4). The report went on to recommend both vigorous state action in this field – 'standardizing the networks, launching communications satellites, and creating data banks' – and a willingness to decentralize 'when the needed changes require other groups to take the initiative' (Nora and Minc 1981: 6, 9).

Ideas surrounding the 'information society' quickly tran-
scended their roots in utopian idealism and disinterested
social science, and by the 1980s took the form of a distinct
revolutionary doctrine. As Nick Dyer-Witheford (1999:
22–6) has characterized it, this doctrine has seven elemental
beliefs: that the world is in a state of fundamental transi-
tion/upheaval, similar in kind and intensity to that experienced in the shift from agrarian to industrial society in the
nineteenth century; that the crucial resource of the new
society is knowledge/information; that the primary dynamic
force in this revolution/society is technology development
and diffusion; that the generation of wealth in the information economy has eclipsed that of the material/manufactur-
ing economy; that the social transformation accompanying
these technical and economic changes is essentially positive;
that the information revolution – technical, economic
and social – is planetary in scale; that the information
revolution is not only a new phase in human *civilization*
but also an evolutionary step forward for *life itself*. We could
add to this list a firm conviction that the information revolution is irresistible and irreversible. Of course, the primary
technological driver of the information society (and its
rhetoric) was/is the personal computer, which, in the 1980s,
shed its rarity and began its maturation into an everyday mass
appliance.

Theories of the information society thus extended theories
of post-industrialism, modifying them to reflect the rapidly
expanding role played by computing and digitized information in the mediation of an increasing array of social, political and economic activities. As with post-industrialism,
theories heralding the arrival of the information society were
not without critics (Traber 1986). Much of this criticism
questioned the accuracy of labelling as 'revolutionary' a series
of technologically driven dynamics which not only left intact
the foundational logic, practices and relationships of liberal-
democratic capitalism, but also entrenched them. Some critics
argued that the distinction between the information and
industrial economies was a false one, and preferred instead
to regard computerization as simply part of, or at best a
phase-shift within, well-established industrial production
regimes. Others pointed to the failure of this revolution to

redistribute political power and knowledge, or to reconfigure the possibilities of participation in a substantial way, either within or between societies (Leiss 1989). Most fundamentally, it was clear to many observers that the development of new information technologies and practices occurred under the logic of the market, and were simply instrumental to the reproduction of capitalist relations of production more generally, empowering existing elites and perpetuating the disempowerment of the working class (Lyon 1988; Robins and Webster 1988; H. Schiller 1986). The combined effect of these critiques was a growing sensitivity to the ideological and mythological character of the discourse surrounding the information society.

Post-Fordism

The network society thesis is closely connected to the constellation of theories and analyses which arose in the 1980s under the banner of 'post-Fordism' (Amin 1994). The roots of this discourse lie in the Regulation School of political economy, specifically the work of Michel Aglietta (1979) and Alain Lipietz (1987), who sought to provide a model for understanding the historical resilience of the capitalist mode of production. These thinkers rejected the orthodoxies which stipulated that capitalism was a static phenomenon, historically destined to collapse under the weight of its own contradictions. Instead, the Regulation School conceived of capitalism as a succession of 'regimes of accumulation' comprised of complementary production, consumption and regulatory configurations: a regime of accumulation combines a particular way of producing goods, a particular construction of the consumer market for these goods, and a particular role for state regulation of the market economy.

Fordism, the accumulation regime which prevailed from the late nineteenth to the mid-twentieth century, bears the name of Henry Ford, the archetypical American capitalist industrialist, in whose mass production automobile factories – and in the societies which surrounded them – this regime was made manifest. In terms of production processes, the attributes of the Fordist model are well known: mass, often mechanized, production of highly standardized goods in a very rigid and highly segmented process; human labour reduced to the repetitive execution of highly circumscribed, specialized, routinized tasks which admitted little variation or discretion on the part of the labourer; the replacement of individual judgement and craft by standardized operational principles oriented to maximum efficiency (i.e. the application of Taylorist principles of 'scientific management').

Fordist relations of production featured large numbers of relatively interchangeable wage-labourers gathered into urban masses proximate to sites of production, disciplined variously by the punitive wrath of middle-class managers, the persistent prospect of unemployment, and collective agreements negotiated between capitalists and trade unions. Interestingly, while trade unionism and collective bargaining were institutionalized through this period, in many cases the very qualities which enabled unions to achieve some modicum of security for working people also complemented the organizational logic of the Fordist accumulation regime: strict hierarchy and bureaucratization; rigid, specialized job classifications; separation of the interests of the employed and the unemployed; and a repudiation of radicalism (Harvey 1989: 133–4).

The mass production paradigm of the Fordist regime was paralleled by the creation and maintenance of mass markets able to absorb the surfeit of consumer goods yielded by increasingly productive and efficient manufacturing techniques. Fordist enterprises were very good at converting resources into massive quantities of standardized goods efficiently at a relatively low cost, and commuting this efficiency into profits required the consistent generation of demand for those goods. Goods were thus not the only thing manufactured under the regime of Fordism – it also featured close attention to the manufacture of appetite for these goods; the scientific management of labour and the mass production process was complemented by a parallel effort to manage desire in a culture of mass consumption. New communications technologies and industries (i.e. broadcast radio and television) provided media through which a mass culture of consumption could be manufactured, and the quasi-scientific practices of opinion polling, market research and advertising provided means for the management of the mass audience and market (Leiss et al. 1990).

Massive numbers of otherwise discrete individuals could be persuaded by advertisers and Hollywood that they all needed the same cigarettes and automobiles, but profitability under the Fordist regime also required that these masses actually be able to purchase the goods they had been induced to desire. Ensuring this entailed balancing the gains to be made by keeping labour costs low (via automation and low wages) with the need to maintain acceptable levels of purchasing power amongst the consuming class. The crucial role of demand management under the Fordist regime also required that the capitalist state be prepared to intervene to offset cyclical market failures and restore equilibrium. The activist Keynesian welfare state – the definitive state form of the Fordist accumulation regime – accomplished this in a number of ways, including income redistribution, unemployment insurance, labour and market regulation, collectivization of mass education and healthcare costs, and counter-cyclical public spending to prop up demand in times of recession. The centralized, regulatory state completed the Fordist regime by providing stable conditions for mass production and mass consumption within territorially defined national units.

Looking backwards, it could be argued that the first signs of instability in the Fordist regime were the countercultural social movements of the late 1960s, many of which rejected – either explicitly or implicitly – the spirit of mass society. By the mid-1970s, the economic and political foundations of Fordism were coming under similar strain: domestic markets in the advanced economies were reaching saturation, which led to sometimes forcible and politically contentious penetration into foreign markets in search of untapped demand for consumer items; downward pressure on employment and wage levels led to increasing labour unrest and strikes, which in turn led many manufacturers to relocate production operations to jurisdictions where labour was less organized, undercompensated and more easily managed; rising unemployment and inflation outpaced the ability of most welfare states to compensate and stabilize demand. Crucially, during this period it was also becoming more difficult for states to redistribute the diminishing fruits of Fordist prosperity, or to provide the levels of general welfare (i.e., housing, health care, education) upon which the legitimacy of the Keynesian social contract rested.

The response of capitalist elites and the capitalist state to this crisis can be captured in a single word: *flexibility* – the word most closely associated with the post-Fordist regime of accumulation, and a word that continues to occupy a place of privilege in the economic discourse of the network society (Harvey 1989: 140–72; Piore and Sabel 1984). Drawing direction from the success of east Asian (particularly Japanese) economies in weathering the economic storm of the 1970s, European and North American economies began to restructure with an eye to building flexibility into each of the three elements of the accumulation regime.

Thus, in the realm of production, the flexibilities of so-called 'Toyotism' gradually replaced the rigidity of Fordist mass manufacturing: economies of scale were replaced by economies of scope (i.e., elimination of large inventories in favour of 'just-in-time' delivery of specialized orders); small batch production of variable product types replaced mass production of standardized goods; integration of production from initiation to finishing and individual multitasking replaced task segmentation; limited individual judgement, craft and skill were reintroduced; Taylorist hierarchical management structures and standardization of operational processes were modified by the flattening of hierarchies and limited decentralization of decision-making by 'teams' with increased discretion, better knowledge of the scope of the enterprise, and enhanced responsibility for the 'quality' of productive output. This reconfiguration of the productive process necessitated a parallel restructuring of the relations of production and the Fordist industrial workforce: the fully employed mass proletariat was reconfigured into a small and shrinking core group of highly skilled workers and a larger, growing group of non-traditional employment categories (self-employed subcontractors, short-term contract employees, temporary workers, freelancers, part-timers, job sharers, teleworkers). In concert with these shifts has been a dismantling of established, well-defined job classifications and working conditions/compensation arrangements, and a high degree of volatility, insecurity and liquidity in the labour market. Additionally, qualification in relatively static craft and skill sets has given way to continuous retraining in response to technological innovation in work processes. Together, these measures dramatically increased the flexibility with which labour could be deployed in relation to economic fluctuations and market conditions. Needless to say, this occupational and labour market restructuring was accompanied by decreasing rates of unionization, as well as a diminishing level of power on the part of organized workers and their representatives relative to that which they enjoyed under the Fordist regime – despite the rhetoric of individual and 'team' empowerment that attended these changes.

Just as mass consumption complemented the mass productivity of the Fordist regime, so too does the flexible specialization of post-Fordism have a complementary ethic of consumption in what has been characterized as pluralized or individualized consumption behaviour. That the new consumption regime is often described contradictorily as 'mass customization' reveals both the realities of scale which linger on in advanced economies despite the eclipse of Fordism, as well as the discursive cunning of the post-Fordist solution to market saturation and exhaustion. Manufacturers in large economies continue to generate massive quantities of consumer goods and services that are more standardized than they are customized – nevertheless some degree of variation in the properties of these goods, particularly when this variation can be rapidly responsive to consumer preferences within a defined range, has proved to be an effective technique for the regeneration and management of demand. Just as the Fordist regime relied on the manufacture of a culture of mass consumption, the post-Fordist regime relies on the continual manufacture of a culture where consumption is at least perceived to be customized, pluralized and specialized. Thus, for example, instead of producing a single type of computer with a fixed set of universal features and marketing this to a single mass of consumers by manufacturing in that mass a homogeneous need, it is now more prudent to produce computers whose attributes can be chosen from within a certain range by a plurality of consumers. Provided that production processes are sufficiently flexible to meet this degree of specialization, the consumption behaviour encouraged under the post-Fordist regime presents to firms the possibility of a market that continually reproduces itself simply by expressing superficial preferences.

The role of the state under the post-Fordist regime of accumulation is essentially to provide the conditions for flexibility, innovation and competitiveness. Typified by the Thatcher government in the United Kingdom, the Reagan administration in the United States and the Mulroney government in Canada, the post-Fordist state bears little resemblance to its Keynesian forebear. Many of the positions characteristic of these states could be characterized as a retreat of the public role of the state in economic matters. These have included rapid privatization of state enterprises; market deregulation; decentralization of state authority; lowering barriers to the mobility of capital and labour; decreased taxation; and privatization/devolution of social welfare and security delivery. On the other hand, post-Fordist states have played more activist roles in crafting anti-inflationary fiscal and monetary policy, subsidizing research and development pursuant to innovation, funding and constructing the technological infrastructure for enterprise, creating the regulatory conditions for the flexible deployment of labour, and fabricating attractive investment environments to offset the flight of highly mobile capital. The latter set of policies would seem to undermine the ideological fiction that the post-Fordist state is somehow less activist under these new economic conditions, and to suggest rather that the state continues to act, only using different techniques towards somewhat modified ends.

Thus, to recap, the post-Fordist regime of accumulation is said to have accomplished the following transitions: from Taylorism and mass production to flexible specialization; from the mass proletariat to a more flexible labour market; from mass, standardized consumption to pluralized customization; and from the Keynesian welfare state to the neo-liberal competitive state. Theories of post-Fordism have been subject to a variety of criticisms, including charges that they overemphasize discontinuities in capitalist development at the expense of continuities, that they uncritically accept the propaganda of the business elite regarding enterprise restructuring as evidence of a fundamental shift in the organization of work, that they are technologically determinist, and that they are more concerned with theorizing the continued stability of capitalism than its inherent irrationality and injustice (Pollert 1991). Nevertheless, the dynamics described by the post-Fordist analysis remain central to the network society thesis.

Postmodernism

A fourth discourse that is intimately linked with the network society thesis is that of postmodernism, a notoriously slippery and often obscure collection of theoretical positions that emerged from the writing of leftist intellectuals in France following the student–worker uprisings in the spring of 1968, and subsequently has been elaborated across a broad range of disciplines in the arts, social sciences and humanities (Best and Kellner 1991; Rosenau 1992). The work of writers such as Michel Foucault, Jacques Derrida, Jean-François Lyotard, Jean Baudrillard, Gilles Deleuze and Felix Guattari resonated deeply with the rapidly changing social and economic conditions of the era (Lyon 1994) and inspired a fundamental challenge to the basic categories of Western social and political thought.

As its label suggests, postmodernism comes *after* modern political thought, but this does not mean that it is particularly *anti*-modern, as is sometimes supposed. Indeed, it might be more accurate to describe postmodern thought as *hyper*-modern. At the core of modern political thought lies Thomas Hobbes's assertions that truth and falsehood are a function of names rather than nature, and that power rather than justice is the central preoccupation of political life. Friedrich Nietzsche, whose thought represents the culmination of modern political philosophy, declared that Western society had reached a point where it was 'beyond good and evil' and where moral categories such as these, and truth itself, were rightly understood as historical artefacts contingent upon the operation of human will-to-power. Postmodern thinkers seized on these elements of modern political theory to radically undermine traditional notions of the constitution of truth and reality. In the postmodern view, truth is neither metaphysical unity nor correspondence to the observed material world; it is instead simply the regularized and institu-

tionalized product of human discourse, which is itself an
outcome of the operation of power in human relationships.
As such, the truth is not a transhistorical, stable standard in
light of which practices can be consistently judged; it is rather
the deeply historical and contested outcome of those practices themselves – a reflection, rather than a source, of power.

This view of the nature of the truth – what we might label
the postmodern *epistemology* or account of knowledge –
gives rise to a gamut of concerns and positions which characterize the broader agenda of postmodernism. Common to
most postmodern approaches to the study of social phenomena is a heightened awareness of the constructive function of
language, and the manner in which language itself encodes
and legitimates particular practices and relationships in a
given historical context. In this view political struggles are,
at their root, textual struggles over language and discourse,
and the task of thought is to deconstruct prevailing discursive configurations to reveal the radical contingency at their
centre (Derrida 1974). In particular, postmodernists have
sought to undermine or at least destabilize the so-called
'grand' or 'meta-' narratives of history which purport to
express something unifying about the human condition (i.e.,
the historical narratives of Progress, Reason, Enlightenment,
Liberty, Class Struggle, etc.) but which in fact do violence to
the irreducible particularity of human existence by silencing
micro-narratives that are marginal to the story imagined by
whichever master narrative happens to be operative at any
given time. Thus, postmodernists position themselves as
champions of the silenced, marginal, 'little' or 'micro-' narratives against the totalizing tendencies of the hegemonic,
'grand' or 'meta-' narratives (Lyotard 1984).

The postmodern assertion of the discursive and narrative
qualities of truth has also been elaborated into a set of
provocative claims about the status of reality itself. Language,
in this view, is not only constructive in its function, but also
highly self-referential – as opposed to representational – in
operation. That is to say, more than to any concrete objective reality out there in the world, language most often refers
to itself; language does not simply represent or symbolize the
world, it constitutes a complicated code in which certain elements are internally connected but not obviously linked to

any external, objective reality. Radical postmodernists have seized on this notion to suggest that the status of so-called reality is highly unstable, communicable only through highly subjective applications of symbolic codes that decreasingly refer to any stable ground outside language. Thus, social and political life is now enacted in the realm of hyper-reality, a realm of intense simulation where symbolic exchange no longer refers to an objective reality that is external to that exchange – a world of copies of copies with no original referents, where language no longer simulates reality but rather marks its complete absence as a meaningful category (Baudrillard 1983). This notion of *hyper*-reality – a world of discourse that floats *beyond*, and is indistinguishable from, reality – has had strong purchase in the media-saturated cultures of the affluent West.

Perhaps the closest connection between theories of post-modernism and the network society thesis arises in the context of anti-essentialist conceptions of human identity. Just as postmodernists reject fixed foundations for the truth and stable, objective grounds for claims about reality, so too do they question the premise that there is a relatively stable, coherent, unified centre – whether spiritual or biological – which comprises the essence of selfhood and from which human identity directly emerges. Identities, like truth and reality, are constructed through discourse. They are thus built upon shifting relationships and networks of power, expressed in language practices using the materials provided by, and appropriated in, distinct social, cultural and political config-urations. Human identity is thus contested, contextual, multiple, fragmentary and transient – human beings construct multiple selves which appear in sometimes incoherent and contradictory combinations, dependent on contexts which themselves often overlap or are seemingly incommensurable. The self-reflective postmodernist does not ask, *what am I?* Instead s/he asks, *who, or which combination of my selves, am I today, here, in this context*, and *what is it that makes me that and not someone else?* In this view, rather than some-thing deep and unalterable, the self or identity is the discur-sive surface upon which a complex network of relationships, symbols and gestures converge to articulate themselves. The question this raises for social or political analysis is that of figuring out which particular identities are normalized in particular contexts and which are marginalized, and under which constellations of power or conventions of discourse they are assigned that status.

Globalization

The final set of ideas relevant as a foreground to our discussion of the network society coheres around the theme of globalization, which became commonplace in the 1990s. At the core of all theories of globalization is the claim that nation-states are being challenged in their capacity to organize and contain core elements of modern economic, political and social life. The source of this challenge has been a historical dynamic of deterritorialization in each of these three realms: economic activities once relatively contained within national borders are now prosecuted as if borders were non-existent; state political authority once limited only by national geographic boundaries now finds itself also challenged and hedged by international and transnational (sometimes regional, sometimes global) regimes; social practices, identities and solidarities once defined by national purposes and parameters are decreasingly characterized or contained in this way. Correlated with these challenges to the containment capacity of national states is a dynamic of accelerated mobility or 'flow' – of people, commodities, technology and information – across borders. In most analyses, these conditions are described in terms of *decline*: a decline of national economies; a decline of national political sovereignty; a decline of nationally defined social identity and culture.

Economic considerations figure centrally in most accounts of globalization. The historical tendency of capitalist economic activity towards organization and operation at the level of the nation-state has given way in the latter decades of the twentieth century to a centrifugal reconfiguration of capitalism as a transnational phenomenon. This transnationalization has occurred at every level of advanced capitalism. In terms of the mode of production – the foundation of any economy – contemporary capitalism is increasingly organized and executed beyond national contexts, with production chains, material resourcing, labour pools and strategic ventures straddling multiple and shifting locations across a plurality of national contexts (Ohmae 1990). It is now not uncommon for raw resources from one country to be synthesized in a second into production materials, which are manufactured in a third into components, which are assembled into finished products in a fourth. The transnationalization of production has been driven by the basic desire to take advantage of the most profitable conditions (i.e., regulatory controls, taxation regimes, labour costs) for productive activities in any given moment regardless of location – a desire facilitated when the economic penalties for relocation are relaxed and technologies which enable management and coordination of geographically disaggregated operations are readily available. Complementing this transnationalization of production have been increases in both global trade and foreign direct investment. In 1997, the United Nations Development Program reported that by the mid-1990s global trade had grown to $4 trillion per year, and foreign direct investment reached a level of $315 billion (United Nations Development Program 1997). Finance and capital circulation have similarly escaped the constraints of national systems. A number of factors have contributed to the global integration of finance capital: deregulation and liberalization of domestic controls on the flow of capital after the collapse in 1971 of the Bretton Woods agreement on a fixed exchange-rate system in favour of floating exchange rates; invention of a range of new instruments of speculation and investment; and generalization of technologies capable of mediating and coordinating financial transactions globally, on a 24-hour basis. By 1995, global trading in foreign currencies had surpassed a volume of $1.2 trillion (US) *per day* (United Nations Development Program 1997). Early in its development, Susan Strange coined the phrase 'casino capitalism' to name this new, transnational finance economy (Strange 1986), and later she described the speculative, globally circulating currency driving it as 'mad money' (Strange 1998).

A crucial element of this global restructuring of capitalism has been the rise, since the Second World War, of several international and supranational agreements, instruments and institutions charged with managing the mercurial flow of people, commodities and currencies across national borders. The Bretton Woods conference of 1944 (named for the New Hampshire town where it was held) led to the establishment of two institutions – the International Monetary Fund (IMF) and the World Bank – whose purpose was to regulate various aspects of the emerging system of international capitalism (Cohn 2000). Initially, the role of the IMF was to provide short-term loans to bolster the fixed exchange rates of currencies in countries experiencing temporary balance of payment problems; when the system of fixed rates collapsed in the early 1970s, the IMF shifted its emphasis to managing Third World debt. The World Bank was formed to provide long-term loans for postwar reconstruction in Europe; however when much of this reconstruction was instead financed through bilateral aid packages (i.e., the United States's Marshall Plan) the World Bank turned its attention to economic development in the Third World. In 1947, twenty-three industrialized countries signed the General Agreement on Tariffs and Trade, a structure for opening and managing trade in goods between signatories that was succeeded in 1995 by the World Trade Organization (WTO), whose mandate extended to liberalizing trade in services, intellectual property, and trade-related investment. Still another international body active in this area is the Organization for Economic Cooperation and Development (OECD – the core of which is known as the G8), founded in 1961 as a forum in which industrial nation-states could develop coordinated approaches to common economic problems. The OECD has been a major player in the move to eliminate barriers to the free flow of goods and capital across borders, as exemplified in its drafting and promotion of the ill-fated Multilateral Agreement on Investment (MAI). Supplementing – or perhaps embodying – the work of these institutions has been the proliferation of a range of regional trade and investment organizations (Asia-Pacific Economic Cooperation; Association of Southeast Asian Nations (ASEAN); European Economic and Monetary Union) and bilateral and multilateral regional free-trade agreements (North American Free Trade Agreement; Southern Common Market Treaty (Mercosur); ASEAN Free Trade Area), which together purport to transform the international economy into a global marketplace.

One political consequence of this global liberalization of the capitalist economy has been a deterioration of nation-states' ability to unilaterally manage their economic activities according to exclusively domestic priorities (McGrew and Lewis 1992). States still make and enforce decisions, but they do so in an environment in which their possible courses of action are increasingly hedged by conditions set by international economic institutions and agreements such as those listed above. Whether it is a Third World nation grudgingly conforming to 'structural adjustment' requirements in order to qualify for an IMF loan, or an industrial nation whose efforts to support indigenous industry are deemed an unfair trade and investment practice, the rules of the game of the global economy lead states either to take actions they might not have otherwise, or to refrain from actions and policies they might otherwise have freely chosen to undertake. Sacrificing a certain degree of political autonomy is a condition of admission into the global economy, wherein states compete for market share, rather than for territory. Many see in this sacrifice a decline of the sovereignty of nation-states, as they essentially transfer a great deal of their authority to disembodied agreements and conventions, to largely unaccountable institutions dominated by ruling interests from a narrow selection of wealthy states (the IMF and World Bank have voting systems weighted in favour of rich states, who also set the agendas and dominate the leadership of the WTO and OECD), and to the transnational corporations which find themselves relatively unconstrained in this environment. Under these conditions, states decreasingly resemble centralized bodies capable of enforcing sovereign authority *within* the boundaries of their respective territories, and begin to act more like 'transmission belts' that facilitate the movement of goods and capital *through* their jurisdictions (Cox 1987).

These dynamics have led to the widespread perception that globalization names a set of phenomena that are deeply un- and anti-democratic, constituting a disconnection between the locus of effective power (to the extent such a locus exists in a globalized condition) and the site of citizenship, representation and accountability. In the modern context, these democratic categories have customarily been organized in correspondence with effective political and economic power at the level of the sovereign nation-state. However, as the political and economic authority of nation-states is restructured and transferred, the organization of democratic citizenship, representation and accountability around national institutions loses its effectiveness. Absent the institutionalization of meaningful citizenship opportunities, effective representation, and legitimate accountability in parallel with the globalization of economic and political power, a democratic crisis ensues. The manifestations of this crisis – captured well in Lou Pauly's provocative question, *Who Elected the Bankers?* (1997) – range from declining rates of participation in national elections across the liberal democracies, to the trivialization of national politics reduced to scandal and spectacle, to the increasingly violent mass demonstrations which now routinely attend meetings of the various international agencies identified as the vanguard of globalization. It is important to be careful not to exaggerate the demise of the sovereignty of nation-states: state governments retain considerable and significant discretion in the formulation and execution of domestic social-policy regimes and even economic-policy regimes and, after all, it is national governments which form, direct and consent to the activities of international agencies and agreements. In light of this, it is worth bearing in mind that while the neo-liberal marketization at the heart of globalization is often taken to signal a retreat of governance, the construction and maintenance of these markets are ever and always the result of policy choices consciously taken by sovereign state governments, choices that could have been made differently. States participate, with varying degrees of willingness and enthusiasm, in the establishment and maintenance of market conditions that allow transnational economic actors to operate and prosper. It is also the case that new structures of global governance – as well as globally organized and globally concerned political movements – are slowly emerging (Held 1995). Whether these will satisfy the democratic aspirations of global citizens remains to be seen.

The dynamics of globalization operate in the cultural arena as well, as the material and practices of identity and community are deterritorialized, and flow across geopolitical borders with increasing ease (Appadurai 1996). Just as the nation-state's role as a container for political and economic activity has declined, so too has its ability to contain identity, community and culture. Several factors have combined to produce the condition of 'postnationalism' that is often associated with globalization: dramatically increased international migration and a concomitant proliferation of multiethnic societies and diasporic communities; the rise of media technologies which facilitate the global distribution and consumption of mass cultural products, as well as inexpensive, timely, interpersonal communication across vast distances; and the diminishing ability of states to protect and nurture domestic, indigenous cultural industries in the context of the global, liberalized market conditions described above (which pertain to cultural goods and practices when they take the form of intellectual property and are commodified).

It is certain that, in the contemporary context, these dynamics have combined to succeed in detaching the phenomenon of culture from its concentration in a particular geographic location. Nevertheless, the implications of cultural globalization are hotly contested. From one perspective, it is argued that globalization constitutes the culmination of modern deracination, the final stage in the progressive homogenization of meaningful cultural distinctions into a single, mass consumer culture emanating from the conglomerated, transnational media empires of the United States. In this view, globalization is a particularly virulent strain of American cultural imperialism enabled by the political economy of late capitalism, and is synonymous with the demise of national, cultural particularities. From another perspective, however, the view is less bleak. In this view, globalization names a phenomenon of cultural heterogeneity and hybridization, in which immigrant communities bring their cultures with them, maintaining and mixing these with the cultures of their new homes, and in which globally dispersed recipients of Western mass cultural products appropriate these in creative and idiosyncratic ways, to craft identities that negotiate between the local and the cosmopolitan (Cheah and Robbins 1998). Here, coherent cultures grounded in territorially bounded nations have certainly suffered under the flows of globalization, but this is not seen as cause for despair.

On this account, it is at least conceivable that the open-ended cultural cross-fertilization embodied in globalization is more natural, healthy and liberating than the somewhat artificial construct of insulated national culture could ever be.

The network society

The concept of the network society, and certainly the range of phenomena it attempts to describe, encompasses numerous elements of the five discourses briefly summarized above. This is not to say the network society thesis somehow culminates efforts over the past several decades to name the world as it has become at the close of the twentieth century. It is not – whether as a name or as a condition – the 'successor' to post-industrialism, the information society, post-Fordism, postmodernism and/or globalization. It is, rather, one star among these others in a constellation of relatively recent attempts to understand and characterize an evolving range of interrelated social, political, economic and cultural forces. It demands our attention because at present it is arguably the brightest of these stars, but it should come as no surprise that the conditions and relationships described by the network society thesis closely resemble those encountered in the five theoretical discourses discussed above. That being said, the idea of the network society does add something particular and distinctive to this conversation.

The phrase 'network society' applies to societies that exhibit two fundamental characteristics. The first is the presence in those societies of sophisticated – almost exclusively digital – technologies of networked communication and information management/distribution, technologies which form the basic infrastructure mediating an increasing array of social, political and economic practices. A detailed discussion of these technologies will be the subject of the next chapter. The second, arguably more intriguing, characteristic of network societies is the reproduction and institutionalization throughout (and between) those societies of *networks* as the basic form of human organization and relationship across a wide range of social, political and economic configurations and associations. The remainder of the present chapter will be devoted to elaborating the nature of the network form and the broad attributes of the societies to which it lends shape.

Networks

Networks are comprised of three main elements: nodes, ties and flows. A node is a distinct point connected to at least one other point, though it often simultaneously acts as a point of connection between two or more other points. A tie connects one node to another. Flows are what pass between and through nodes along ties. To illustrate, we might consider a group of friends as a network: each friend is a *node*, connected to at least one other friend but typically to many others who are also connected, both independently and through one another; the regular contacts between these friends, either in speech or other activities, whether immediate or mediated by a technology, are the *ties* that connect them; that which passes between them – gossip, camaraderie, support, love, aid – are *flows*.

Attached to each of these three elements is a number of variables which, taken together, condition the character of any given network. Nodes (e.g., friends, computers, firms) can be powerful or powerless, active or dormant, stationary or mobile, permanent or temporary, net sources or net recipients of various kinds of flows. Ties (e.g., correspondence, cables, contracts) can be strong or weak, private or public, singular or multiple, unique or redundant, sparse or dense, parallel or intersecting. Flows (e.g., gossip, data, money) can be copious or minimal, constant or intermittent, one-way or reciprocal, uni- or multidirectional, balanced or imbalanced, meaningful or meaningless. Depending on which of these and other variable characteristics its constituent elements bear, a network can exhibit a number of qualities. Networks can be centralized, decentralized (i.e., multicentred), or distributed (i.e., centreless); hierarchical or horizontal; bounded or boundless; finite (i.e., with fixed limits on the number of nodes and ties) or proliferating (i.e., with no limit on the number of nodes and ties); accessible or inaccessible; inclusive or exclusive; intensive (i.e., few nodes linked by a multiplicity of dense, strong ties) or expansive (i.e., many nodes linked by relatively sparse, weak ties); interactive (i.e. enabling reciprocal, multidirectional flows) or non-interactive (i.e. enabling only one-way, uni-directional flows).

The network society thesis suggests that an increasing number of contemporary social, political and economic practices, institutions and relationships are organized around the network form – flows between nodes connected by ties – though the precise configuration and character of these networks vary depending on how they combine the variable qualities of these three essential elements. These combinations will depend heavily upon the material and discursive conditions (i.e. the historical contexts) in which these networks are situated, though it is also true that the network form introduces new organizational possibilities for human associations and institutions, some of which may strain against the very conditions from which these networks emerge.

Attributes of the network society

In Castells's formulation, 'the network society . . . is made up of networks of production, power and experience, which construct a culture of virtuality in the global flows that transcend time and space' (Castells 1998: 370). The network society – the society in which the network form of organization replaces other forms, across the categories of politics, economics and culture – bears the marks of many of the dynamics discussed above in relation to other discourses that have arisen to name the prevailing conditions of late capitalism, liberal democracy and international relations. It is also true that consideration of the centrality of the network form adds something distinctive to these attempts to capture and identify the spirit of the present age. The network society thesis, then, at once gathers and augments many of the themes discussed in this chapter. In his pathbreaking formulation of this thesis, Castells isolates a number of attributes that together give shape to the network society (Castells 1998). Before proceeding to discuss these in detail in the ensuing chapters, it would be useful to briefly summarize them here.

At the economic base of the network society is an 'informational' – *as opposed to strictly industrial* – *capitalist economy.* These are economies that have been restructured to reflect the primacy of the generation and distribution of knowledge and information, especially as they pertain to the optimization and control of productive processes and markets. They are also economies which emphasize continuous technological innovation and flexibility over maximization of output as the key source of growth (Castells 1996: 14–19). The informational mode of development drives the expansive and rejuvenated form of capitalism at the heart of the network society.

The economy of the network society is organized globally, on the network model. In the network society, capital and commodities (including information commodities) are decreasingly contained within the fixed boundaries of territorially defined nation-states, and instead flow with increasing ease along ties that reach across or through these boundaries, between nodes (i.e., firms, regions, markets) which are often themselves organized as networks. Labour remains more territorially confined than either capital or commodities, though the combination of increasing migration and the flexibility of networked production processes mitigates this, primarily in ways that increase the power and control of capital vis-à-vis labour. No longer primarily organized nationally, the global economy assumes the form of a network of networks linked by information and communication technologies configured on the same model, a model which ramifies throughout the economy, as regions, cities, firms, enterprises, workplaces and even individual workers are reconstituted as flexible, temporary networks of nodes of varying power. As Castells observes, in a post-Fordist, globalized economy, the logic of networks 'structure[s] the unstructured while preserving flexibility' (Castells 1996: 62). One result, of course, is a relative decline in the capacity of the nation-state to organize political, economic and social power in the network society.

In the network society, human experience of time and space is displaced to 'timeless time' and the 'space of flows'

(Castells 1998: 1). Human beings live inextricably in space and time, but our experience of these can vary considerably, especially when mediated and rendered artificial by technology. Naturally, human beings experience time as a recurrence of organic cycles (i.e., bodily rhythms, alternating days and nights, seasons) at rates specific to particular locations, and space as the extent of their regular inhabitation (i.e., where they live) and the distance over which they can reasonably travel, communicate or see. Combined, these experiences of time and space as essentially limiting elicit a sense of 'place' that localizes the organization and coordination of the common activities of human communities. Technological mediation – the standardization of time measurement by clocks, calendars and zones; development of transportation and communication technologies – extends the limits of place, enabling the artificial constitution and coordination of communities on a scale (i.e., the nation-state) greater than was possible under the localizing constraints of nature (Anderson 1983). In the network society, with significant social, political and economic activity increasingly concentrated on flows of information, and with the proliferation of technologies that enable widespread communication of large volumes of information across vast territories instantaneously, the human experience of time and space as essentially localized is nearly obliterated. Computerized networks introduce unprecedented levels of speed, automation and reach into human communication, which decrease the need to synchronize and localize activity in a particular place. Localized experience of time and place – the constraint of place – no longer limits the growing volume of increasingly significant human activity expressed in the communication of information via global network media. The network society is 'always on' and the placement of its members in territorial space is less important than their existence in the 'space of flows' where crucial economic and other activity occurs. It is in this sense that the human beings experience time in the network society as timeless, and space as placeless. In cultural terms, one effect of this dynamic is the generation of a globalized (albeit with regional variations) mainstream consumer culture, constructed by a pervasive and globally integrated media system, which, while superficially hybridizing and incorporating some elements of diverse international cultures, remains highly inorganic, dislocated, and hyper-real. The culture of the timeless, placeless network society exists everywhere, but comes from nowhere; in provocative postmodern phrasing, Castells labels it a 'culture of real virtuality' (Castells 1998: 1).

In the network society, power and powerlessness are a function of access to networks and control over flows. In a society whose principal economic, political and social activities are organized as – or mediated by – networks, access to those networks constitutes an important threshold of inclusion and exclusion, a condition of power and powerlessness, a source of dominance and subjugation. As Castells writes: 'networks also act as gatekeepers. Inside the networks, new possibilities are relentlessly created – outside the networks, survival is increasingly difficult'; and, similarly, 'Presence or absence in the network and the dynamics of each network *vis-à-vis* others are critical sources of domination and change in our society . . .' (Castells 1996: 171, 469). Access to significant networks (i.e., status as a node) is a minimum condition of social, economic and political membership in the network society, and lack of access both reflects and reproduces disenfranchisement, but this is not to say that mere access constitutes empowered membership or equality. As mentioned previously, the network society model contemplates that, in the network of networks (technological, financial, commercial, political, social, etc.) that forms the fabric of a society, some networks and nodes (and therefore connection to these) will be more powerful than others. Some networks will mediate structurally significant activity (e.g., financial networks) while others will mediate activity that is relatively insignificant in structural terms (e.g., chat lines). Some nodes will control and originate flows (e.g., multinational mass media conglomerates) while other nodes will primarily receive flows over which they exert only minimal control (e.g., individual consumers). Some nodes (e.g., governments) will be privy to types and volumes of information to which other nodes (e.g., citizens) are not. Finally, some very powerful nodes (i.e., internet service providers and portals) will actually control access to, and use of, network ties and infrastructure by other, less powerful nodes (i.e., individual users). Thus while access is a minimum condition of enfranchisement in the network society, it by no means ensures equality. Indeed, it is a considerable irony of the network society that, for most of its members, securing the minimum condition of inclusion (and thereby averting complete exclusion and the radical powerlessness it would bring) simply grants them access to the infrastructure of their own continued inequality and relative domination.

That being said, the fact remains that economic, political and social agency in the global network society is inextricably tied to inclusion in those networks. Under these conditions, control over access becomes a crucial mechanism of power and domination, and the divide between the included and the excluded constitutes a line of stratification with serious political and material consequences. Perhaps not surprisingly, such stratification is a structural attribute of the network society, whereby entire regions or countries on the periphery of the global economy, or entire classes of people within the core itself, are effectively denied access and thereby excluded from crucial technological, economic, political and social networks. These are what Castells calls the 'black holes of informational capitalism', populated by people deemed non-valuable and irrelevant (i.e., unfit for labour, consumption or legitimation) from the perspective of global capital, people who are 'socially/culturally out of communication with the universe of mainstream society' and who, as a result, have 'no escape from the pain and suffering inflicted on the human condition for those who, in one way or another, enter these social landscapes' (Castells 1998: 161–3).

The principal source of conflict and resistance in the network society is the contradiction between the placeless character of networks and the rootedness of human meaning. As described above, the network society technologically dislocates our experience of important social, political and economic processes, and dislocates power and control over these. This dislocation is at odds with the essential boundedness of life in time and space, and with what appears to be an abiding human need to exercise some degree of localized control over the conditions of living. As Castells points out, in the network society 'most dominant processes, concentrating power, wealth and information, are organized in the space of flows.

Most human experience, and meaning, are still locally based.' Thus, the network society 'shifts the core economic, symbolic and political process away from the realm where social meaning can be constructed and political control can be exercised' (Castells 1997: 124). This suggests that the network society exhibits a deep tension between the abstract placelessness of network mediation and the stubborn desire of human beings to embed their lives in particular places. This unresolved tension, a result of the disjuncture between globalizing technology and local identity, evinces a condition of alienation described by Castells as a conflict between 'the net and the self' (Castells 1996). It is this conflict which animates several of the most significant social and political antagonisms of the network society. These take numerous tangible forms, and include a range of movements to re-establish local (which, in a globalized world, sometimes means national), democratic control over political, economic, cultural and environmental conditions. Interestingly – in what is yet another irony of the current age – many of these movements are themselves organized (sometimes internationally) on the network model, using sophisticated network technologies.

Conclusion: The spirit of informationalism

No name ever represents the whole of that which it names. This is especially so in the case of names for social formations or epochs. Nevertheless, a name should at least suggest something that is of primary and/or widespread significance in the actual societies to which it is attached. At most, a name will illuminate the spirit, or animating principle, particular to a historically specific time and place. It is a bonus if the name provokes critical reflection on the principle it articulates. The remainder of this book will reflect on whether 'the network society' meets these standards in regard to the global society bridging the twentieth and twenty-first centuries. The ensuing chapters will provide a more detailed investigation of the technologies, economics, politics and social practices gathered under this name.

This chapter began with a discussion of Max Weber's provocative identification of the spirit of modernity with spiritlessness. What, beyond this, is the spirit of the network society? Manuel Castells has isolated an 'ethical foundation of the network enterprise' which he calls 'the spirit of informationalism' (Castells 1996: 199). It exists, he says, in the common cultural code that glues together the various networks which together comprise contemporary societies. His characterization of this spirit merits extended quotation:

> It is made of many cultures, many values, many projects, that cross through the minds and inform the strategies of the various participants in the networks, changing at the same pace as the network's members, and following the organizational and cultural transformation of the units of the network. It is a culture indeed, but a culture of the ephemeral, a culture of each strategic decision, a patchwork of experiences and interests, rather than a charter of rights and obligations. It is a *multi-faceted, virtual culture* ... It is not a fantasy, it is a material force because it informs, and enforces, powerful economic decisions at every moment in the life of the network. But it does not stay long: it goes onto the computer's memory as raw material of past successes and failures. The network enterprise learns to live within this virtual culture. Any attempt at crystallizing the position on the network as a cultural code in a particular time and space sentences the network to obsolescence, since it becomes too rigid for the variable geometry of informationalism. The 'spirit of informationalism' is the culture of 'creative destruction' accelerated to the speed of the optoelectronic circuits that process its signals. (Castells 1996: 199)

There are, in this articulation, echoes of each of the five discourses – post-industrialism, the information society, post-Fordism, postmodernism and globalization – sketched earlier as precursors or companions to the network society thesis. There is also, however, a note that is clearly distinctive. This book might well be described as an exercise in listening for that note in the mercurial technological, economic, social and political practices which define our present situation.

2
Network Technology

The network society is a technological society. In this respect it can be understood as extending – as opposed to departing from – one of the fundamental historical trajectories of modern Western societies. There is, of course, considerable debate about the nature and origins of Western modernity, and it would be overly reductionist to present technology as its singular, defining attribute. Nevertheless, it would be similarly unwise to minimize the role technology, and its animating spirit, have played in the development of modern economies, politics and social life. Early in the seventeenth century, Francis Bacon proposed that human beings liberate scientific knowledge from the grip of speculative philosophy and harness it instead to the 'improvement of their estate, and an increase in their power over nature' (Bacon 1900: subsection 52). Mastery of the concrete world through practical application of science could restore partially the dominion over Creation lost to man in his Fall from innocence. Thus was the technological project of modernity born – a project joined with relative uniformity across the differences of nation, interest and ideology that have otherwise historically divided the societies of the modern West. As Andrew Feenberg has pointed out, in the modern West socialists and capitalists, totalitarians and democrats have all typically 'cheered on the engineers, heroic conquerors of nature' (Feenberg 1999: vii).

The abstraction that is the 'network society' sprang from this project, and has been constructed around one of its specific concrete products: the networked, digital computer. Thus, to understand the network society it is necessary first to think a little bit about the nature of the relationship between social formation and technology in general, as well as to consider the most significant attributes of this technology in particular. It is to these tasks that the present chapter is devoted. It will begin with a discussion of competing theories of technology, and conclude with an account of the features of contemporary network technology that have emerged in the present context as most significant for the technology's social outcomes and possibilities.

Theories of technology and society

That technology and modern society are mutually embedded is rarely contested; the precise nature of their relationship and mutual influence, on the other hand, typically provokes debate. In crude terms, and in relation to the specific technology under consideration here, this debate can be represented as follows: does society make the internet what it is, or does the internet make society what it is? Alternatively, we could ask: are networked computers just tools, or are they something more, something *technological*? To put it in even more complex terms: are technologies simply means to ends that exist outside and beyond them, or do technologies prescribe ends (as opposed to serving them) or, even, comprise ends in themselves? These tensions are present in the very word 'technology', which combines the ancient Greek words *technē* and *logos*. *Technē* refers to the practical arts, those forms of applied knowledge that, when executed skilfully, typically result in the fabrication of useful things. Emphasis on this part of the word lends itself to understanding technology as a neutral tool or instrument, directed by human practitioners to the achievement of their ends, ends that are independent of the technical means employed to reach them. *Logos* refers to 'the word' or speech, and more broadly denotes a reasoned account of a thing, an account that collects particulars into a rational, coherent whole. Emphasis on this part of the word supports an understanding of technology as a practice that collects people and their activity into a particular way of being in the world, a logic that gathers a particular set of ends and social relations, and as an artefact that materializes an account of that way of being, those ends and relations. The word technology is thus loaded with (at least) two meanings. Debates about the nature of technology and its relation to social practices and formation often turn on the manner in which the tension between these seemingly contradictory meanings is resolved.

Instrumentalism

There is a strain of discourse – arguably the most persistent and commonplace strain – that insists technologies are neutral tools, instruments empty of substance whose outcomes depend entirely upon the uses to which they are put intentionally by human beings. This view is typically styled 'instrumentalism' because it holds that the meaning of technologies is exhausted by their status as instruments, devised by human ingenuity as means to achieve more effectively ends deemed by people to be worthwhile. In this view, the significance of the automobile as a technology resides in its effectiveness as a tool for transporting people from one place to another; the significance of the internet is that it enables the exchange of large volumes of information over considerable distances at great speeds. In the instrumentalist view, technological devices can be employed to achieve a variety of ends (e.g., the internet can mediate democratic citizenship and/or it can mediate illiberal surveillance) and these ends can be adjudged as good or bad, worthwhile or worthless, but not the technologies themselves. Under this paradigm, the only sort of judgement that can be brought to bear against technological devices is a technical appraisal of their *efficiency* in meeting their appointed ends. Technologies are not good or bad, they are efficient or inefficient; moral and political judgement applies to ends, not means. The internet is beyond good and evil, it simply either works or does not.

This is not to say that the instrumentalist view of technology is without moral content. For while it holds fast to the principle that specific technologies are neutral as to ends, it is also part of the distinctly modern tradition that regards technological innovation *in general* as inherently good. The moral silence of instrumentalism with regard to specific technological devices does not extend to the question of technological development as such. On this question, the morality of instrumentalism is quite categorical: technological innovation is thoroughly subsumed under the category of 'progress', an unambiguously good end. Just as Bacon envisioned, the practical application of science to the progress of technology relieves man's estate, makes concrete his mastery over the earth, and contributes to his prosperity. True, technological means can be employed in the service of barbarism and human degradation. However, in these cases it is not technological progress itself that is to be blamed, but rather simply the intentions of those who control its direction, and the conditions under which it unfolds. Even the possibility of unintended and unforeseen harmful consequences does not recommend against pursuing technological progress; rather, these just remind us of human fallibility and motivate us to improve our science, and to be more careful in our calculations. It is also worth noting that the instrumentalist assumptions of technology as neutral and technological progress as good have historically constituted a ground upon which otherwise divergent world-views comfortably meet. Technological progress has, of course, been central to the project of modern liberal capitalism; it also figured highly both in Marxist theory (technology released from the distortions of capitalism and private property would provide for well-distributed freedom from toil) and in the programmes of state socialist regimes.

Substantivism

Despite its hegemony in the modern industrial world, not everyone has been convinced by the instrumentalist account of technology. Accordingly, an alternative discourse has arisen to challenge the assumptions that technology is neutral and its progress an unalloyed good. This view – customarily labelled 'substantivism' and formulated in the Western tradition by the likes of Max Weber (1958), Martin Heidegger (1977), Jacques Ellul (1964), George Grant (1969b) and Albert Borgmann (1984) – maintains that beneath the superficial variety of technological instruments and their applications, technology *as such* has a substantive essence that implicates it in the deepest meaning of human souls, and in the prevailing character of societies where its logic holds sway. Individual devices may indeed be neutral as to their instrumental ends – as George Grant once wrote: 'The computer does not impose on us the ways it must be used' (Grant 1986: 21) – but technology in general embodies and enforces a particular way of being in the world, a particular conception of human relations. To use Heidegger's language, technology *enframes* or, as Grant puts it, technology is 'a whole way of looking at the world, the basic way Western men experience their own existence in the world' (Grant 1969a: 3). Andrew Feenberg, himself a critic of substantivist views, captures their core conviction very well:

> They argue that technology is not neutral but embodies specific values. Its spread is therefore not innocent. The tools we use shape our way of life in modern societies where technique has become all-pervasive. In this situation, means and ends cannot be separated. How we do things determines who and what we are. Technological development transforms what it is to be human. (Feenberg 1999: 2)

It is not just that we make things with particular technological instruments; technology in general also makes something of us.

Consequently, technology admits of (indeed, it demands) moral and political judgement. As if to mirror the moral celebration of technology implicit in the instrumentalist position, substantivist analyses almost always entail radical, and often bleak, moral critiques of technology. Weber's depiction, alluded to in chapter 1 above, of technological modernity as an 'iron cage', and of its captives as 'specialists without spirit; sensualists without heart' (Weber 1958: 182) is embryonic in this regard. Most substantivist accounts identify technology with the empire of instrumental rationality, standardization and homogenization, the celebration of mastery over human and non-human nature (precisely inverting instrumentalist assumptions about the connection between technology and freedom) and the cult of accumulation and efficiency. In substantivist accounts, specific technologies such as the internet are understood as particular moments in which some combination of these attributes, which belong to the essence, spirit or substance of technology, is revealed (Barney 2000: 192–235). In this respect, inventions that might be portrayed under the instrumentalist paradigm as instances of technological innovation or change are typically characterized by substantivist analyses as confirming the continuity of the more fundamental trajectory of technological society. This raises the question, for example, of whether the internet is radically discontinuous, or radically continuous, with the technologies that have preceded it.

Social constructivism

Substantivist theories provide powerful philosophical grounds for a critical approach to modern technological societies, something that is unavailable in instrumentalist approaches. Still, critical theorists of technology have also been careful to point out the limitations of substantivism. In particular, it has been argued that substantivist theories – with their emphasis on the irreducible essence of technology and its disclosure in every technological episode – are overly deterministic. That is to say, substantivist analyses are open to the charge that they treat technology as a monochromatic, autonomous force that is external to, and imposed upon, human social relations. As an autonomous force, so this line of criticism goes, technology is understood as proceeding under its own logic and momentum, and as determining outright and comprehensively the character of the practices it mediates. This criticism pertains, for example, to accounts that maintain the internet is inherently decentralizing and democratizing, as well as those that maintain the internet will necessarily undermine democracy. Critics charge that the deterministic nature of substantivist theories denies the contingency and heterogeneity of actual technological outcomes in the world, and also denies the role of history, culture and human agency in conditioning and effecting these outcomes. In this respect, substantivist theories are open to the charge of mimicking instrumentalism in its effective removal of politics from the determination of technological outcomes in the world. In sum, critics of substantivist approaches to understanding technology argue that it is far too philosophical, and not nearly sociological enough, in its assumptions.

Accordingly, an alternative critical approach has arisen that attempts to avoid the determinist tendencies of substantivism. This approach is known as 'social constructivism' and its origins lie in the sociological and historical analyses of science carried out by thinkers such as Thomas Kuhn (1962), Paul Feyerabend (1975) and Sandra Harding (1991). As its label suggests, the core assumption of the social constructivist approach is that technological outcomes are underdetermined by the essence of technology (if such a thing even exists, a proposition that most social constructivists reject outright) and are, instead, constructed via the interaction between the technology in question, and the social relations/environment in which it is situated (Pinch and Bijker 1990). The principles directing a technological outcome are not necessarily or exclusively the technical rationality and efficiency celebrated by instrumentalists and condemned by substantivists. Instead, a plurality of possibilities exists for any given technology, and which of those possibilities congeals in its eventual outcome depends upon a similarly diverse variety of material and political conditions. As Feenberg writes:

> Constructivists argue that many paths lead out from the first forms of a new technology. Some are well-trodden while others are quickly deserted . . . there are always viable technical alternatives that might have been developed in place of the successful one. The difference lies not so much in the superior efficiency of the successful designs, as in a variety of local circumstances that differentiate otherwise comparable artifacts. Like other institutions, artifacts succeed where they find support in their local environment. (Feenberg 1999: 10)

If a particular technology is developed according to the iron rationale of technical mastery and efficiency, it is not because this represents the inescapable elaboration of the technology's essence, but rather because those ideological priorities either drive the network of actors responsible for setting the conditions of the technology's use, or have been institutionalized in the particular location where that technology is situated – an alternative set of priorities, institutions or other relations could just as well produce an alternative outcome.

Thus, in the constructivist view, the social character of a technology such as the internet will not be universal and homogeneous, comprehensively determined by the logic of its essence as a technology. Rather, the character of the internet is potentially plural and heterogeneous, and will depend upon the social relations and conditions that arise to support particular elaborations of the technology, and deny other possibilities, in any given context. This means that the internet might be many things in many places – perhaps even many things in one place. It also means that the destiny of the internet is no destiny at all: the outcome of this technology will emerge from ongoing contestation and negotiation – i.e., *from politics*, the character of which may vary depending upon the ideological conditions and power relations prevalent in the various locales in which it is situated.

Finally, this perspective introduces the need to be sensitive to dominant, hegemonic articulations of the technology as well as alternative, counter-hegemonic uses and applications. Social constructivism thus purports to reintroduce history, culture, contingency, contestation and politics – in a phrase, *human agency* – back into the study of technology, and recommends sociological and empirical over philosophical and theoretical approaches to that study. Indeed, this is basically the approach favoured by Manuel Castells in his foundational sociological study of the network society where, despite an emphasis on the transformative effects of digital communication networks, he is careful to affirm that 'Of course, technology does not determine society . . . the final outcome depends on a complex pattern of interaction' (Castells 1996: 5). In a subsequent book, Castells suggests that the constructivist approach is particularly appropriate for the internet. As he puts it: 'the Internet is a particularly malleable technology, susceptible of being deeply modified by its social practice, and leading to a whole range of potential social outcomes – to be discovered by experience, not proclaimed beforehand' (Castells 2001: 5). This raises the possibility that there is not, and will not be, any such thing as *the* network society, but rather that there will be many network *societies*, perhaps continuously reinventing and reconfiguring themselves – a prospect that resonates, significantly, with the amorphous character of the network form itself.

A composite view

It is tempting to portray constructivism as the 'common sense' position at which our understanding of the nature of technology has arrived after a century or more of theoretical development. Such a conclusion would be misleading. Notwithstanding the formidable, and sometimes corrective, contribution constructivist studies have made to deepening our appreciation of the dynamics of technology, it is far from clear that this approach is definitive, or invalidates the insights we might continue to draw from other perspectives. Constructivism is instructive, but not perfect. For example, the logical extension of constructivist approaches seems to be pursuit of micro-level studies that are so localized, and so resistant to abstraction and generalization, that they exclude from the outset questions about technology that just might transcend a particular technology's location in a particular situation. There just might be, for example, something socially significant about the internet that pertains *despite* the manner in which it is appropriated and socially constructed in a particular historical or cultural context. This significance might accrue to contingencies of the medium's design, or it might accrue to the substance of the internet as a technology that shares something with all technologies. Whatever the case, in denying the latter possibility outright, social constructivism risks ruling out the 'techno-logical' character of, for example, the internet, as a significant factor in this particular technology's outcome in the world.

The localizing imperative of the constructivist approach also challenges the legitimacy of importing critical normative standards from one cultural or historical context to another. In some respects, this provides an important bulwark against ethnocentrism; it also, however, makes it difficult to locate defensible grounds for a moral or political critique of technological outcomes that are not indigenous to the situation being studied. Constructivism thus risks descent into a form of apolitical and amoral relativism, leaving us able to describe heterogeneous technological outcomes, but unable to say anything critical about them. We may wish not only to describe the variety of digitally mediated communities that characterize the network society, but also to evaluate them according to something other than their own criteria.

Thus, a viable critical theory of technology must affirm what constructivism has taught us: that crude technological determinism is untenable; that technological encounters are deeply political; that the possibility of contestation, contingency and heterogeneity is always present in technological encounters; and that we must pay strict attention to local differences in technological outcomes. Such a theory must also, however, take into account the limitations of this approach and remain open to the insights to be gained from competing perspectives. In particular, it must be sensitive to the role played in technological outcomes by that which unites one technology to another at a very basic level, and by the peculiarities of the design of technical instruments. It must also understand that the critical truth about technology resides somewhere in the dialogue between the universal and the particular, the essential and the contingent. Analyses of technology informed by such a balanced, composite theory of technology must, I think, pay attention to the following four factors: the *essence* or *spirit* of technology, technical *design*, *situation*, and *use*. In what follows I will explore each of these factors, with specific reference to the digital technologies that comprise the concrete, material infrastructure of the network society.

Technological outcomes

Essence of network technology

What is the essence of technology? Though various accounts in the substantivist tradition render it differently, and suggest a range of qualities as definitive of it, it is possible to identify and synthesize some common ideas here. In the first place, it is often argued that technology is essentially *artificial* (as opposed to natural): whatever specific technologies accomplish or do, they always accomplish something through human ingenuity that nature does not or cannot accomplish or provide for on its own, without the intervention of human artifice. It is not natural, for example, to communicate simultaneously with a dozen people separated by thousands of miles, but it is possible technologically via the artificial intervention of the internet. The internet thus shares in the artificial essence of technology in general. Some go so far as to say that the essence of technology is in fact the *exploitation, domination* or *mastery* of nature, human nature included. In Heidegger's view, the essence of technology is to set upon human and non-human nature and demand that they serve as a 'standing-reserve' of resources to be exploited (Heidegger 1977: 17). In a similar formulation, George Grant suggests that the essence of technology is to regard nature as 'the simply dominated', an idea that 'crushes the idea of providence' (Grant 1959: 111, 52). Arguably, such qualities are as essential to digital technologies as they are to any other. The internet is not just artificial and unnatural, it also defies, denies or commands many of the natural obstacles that would otherwise constrain human communication, and conditions us to scoff at such limits. Elsewhere, I have argued that digital technology in general sets upon the world and its inhabitants and enframes them as a 'standing-reserve of bits' ready for exploitation, an essential characteristic of this technology that is unconcealed in, for example, the practices of digitally mediated surveillance and 'data mining' (Barney 2000: 209).

A second characteristic customarily ascribed to the essence of technology is *instrumental rationality*, a type of reasoning in which calculations of the efficiency of means eclipse judgement about the worthiness of ends, and prescribe human behaviour with considerable insistence. Under the regime of instrumental rationality, what matters is that a given procedure or instrument is the most efficient means to its assigned end, and consideration of ends themselves, according other criteria (e.g., justice, fairness, the common good) serves only to undermine efficiency and progress. As Jacques Ellul has characterized it, the essence of technology is *technique*, which he defines as 'the totality of methods rationally arrived at and having absolute efficiency in every field of human activity' (Ellul 1964: xxv). A society in which this mode of reasoning extends into spheres beyond the technical (i.e., into politics, social life, culture, spirituality, etc.) is, for Ellul, a technological society. It is from this essential element of technology that many of the broad characteristics of technological societies draw their justification and nourishment: secularism; technocracy (rule by experts); bureaucratic administration; automation; prescriptivity (reduced human discretion and judgement); and economic and social specialization.

Does network technology share in this aspect of the essence of technology? Some have argued that digital networks represent a departure from the dynamic linking technology to instrumental reason. In such accounts, the flexibility of digital networks occasions an opening rather than a closure of the range of technological possibilities, an expansion of opportunities for a variety of alternative practices not easily subsumed under the regime of technical efficiency (Turkle 1995; Poster 2001). Others have argued that computers elevate instrumental rationality, calculation and efficiency to their apogee. Joseph Weizenbaum argues, for example, that computers have 'reinforced and amplified those antecedent pressures that have driven man to an ever more highly rationalistic view of his society and an ever more mechanistic image of himself' (Weizenbaum 1976: 11). David Bolter concurs, describing the computer as 'the embodiment of the world as the logician would like it to be' (Bolter 1984: 73). It is possible, as Turkle and others have argued, that the *networking* of computers has been decisive in moderating their bias in favour of instrumental reason and calculation. It is just as conceivable, however, that networking has simply extended and deepened this ineradicable quality of computing, a quality also present in the essence of technology more generally. For, despite whatever alternative practices subsist on the margins of mainstream computer and network use, it would be difficult to deny that the primary application of these instruments has been in the service of more efficient systems of control and coordination (Beniger 1986; Robins and Webster 1999), increased efficiency in data collection, calculation and surveillance (Lyon 2001; Whitaker 1999), elevated efficiencies in automation, bureaucracy and management (Rochlin 1997; Zuboff 1988) and, I would also argue, greater prescriptivity in human social practices and relations. It could be argued that the easy comportment of digital networks with such applications derives from the instrumental rationality that resides in their essence as technologies.

A third set of characteristics customarily attributed to the essence of technology is its bias towards *abstraction, universalism* and *standardization*. Technologies not only prescribe ways of doing things, ways of being in the world – they also prescribe ways of doing things that are abstracted from concrete situations in all their variety. Concrete and discrete practices – like how to make bread – can vary from one location to the next, depending on local conditions, traditions and tastes. What technology, such as an automated bread-making machine, does is to facilitate a routine that is not grounded in any particular discrete concrete location; a routine that, because it is abstracted, can be accomplished everywhere, universally. Lack of standardization at a fairly basic level undermines the foundation of technology – standardization is essential to technology, and standardization requires abstraction from the essential pluralism of concrete human practices and situations. This is the crux of a distinction sometimes made between tools and technologies: tools are employed in practices that are locally determined and distinctive; technologies condition routines that are generalized, and which are optimized in operation *despite* local contexts. The automatic bread-making machine is not an oven: it is not open to a diversity of locally generated materials and practices (at least not if it is to operate optimally); instead, it replaces that diversity of practice and material with a standardized regime, for the sake of convenience. The essence of technology is homogeneity and uprootedness. The technology of the bread-making machine is not grounded in any place or tradition. Instead, it is *abstracted* and it is *standardized*: its procedures are universal, and its loaves uniform, despite the concrete particularities, traditions or history of the location in which it is used, and the people who use it. Technologies thus stand in for rooted practices, and it is this quality that is often held responsible for a perceived opposition between technology and authentic culture.

Perhaps digital networks are to human communication what automated bread-making machines are to the baking of bread. There are considerable grounds for disagreement over whether digital technologies are instruments of standardization and homogenization, or instruments of pluralism and local diversity. Many of the frequently repeated claims surrounding these technologies concern their supposedly inherent capacity – because of a network architecture comprised of multiple ties between multiple nodes – to mediate a decentralization, multiplication and diversification, of information sources and communication choices. With every receiver of information via a computer network also a potential producer and distributor of information, it is difficult to conceive how this could be a medium of homogeneity rather than proliferating variety. It is also the case that digital networks are typically understood as crucial to the development of a commercial culture premised on customization and personalization, and flexible, dynamic adaptation to idiosyncratic local conditions and markets – a development often presented as the direct antithesis of standardized, mass markets and culture. Finally, despite the capacity of networks to mediate communication across great expanses of space with great efficiency – potentially eroding the claims that limits of 'place' or location traditionally exert on a person's attention, obligations and activity – it has been argued that one of the most significant outcomes of the rise of networked communication technology is a reconstitution of local identity, interests and power, particularly within cities and regions that constitute 'hubs' in global economic and political networks. Indeed, this 'glocal' metropolitanism has been identified by Castells as among the definitive attributes of the network society (Castells 1996).

Still, there is also no shortage of evidence and argument suggesting that digital technology exhibits the qualities of abstraction, universalism and homogenization identified by substantivists as part of the essence of technology in general. By enabling easy communication across vast distances at great speeds, digital network technology contributes to an erosion of the limitations and conditions location and time otherwise exert on human communicative activities. As Castells has pointed out in elaborating the 'geography of the Internet' (Castells 2001: 207), place still matters in a net-worked world, but primarily because people living in some 'places' have greater access to global networks than do people living in other, less affluent or technologically saturated places. That is to say, people whose physical lives are located in the affluent world are able to transcend their place through the dislocated communication enabled by network access, while people in impoverished locations where network access is either underdeveloped or beyond their means find their communicative lives more place-bound. The same might be said of poor people in otherwise affluent, highly networked places, though statistics clearly indicate much higher rates of internet access in affluent countries than in poorer countries (Norris 2001: 3–94). In other words, people well placed to afford network technology have the privilege of cosmopoli-tan placelessness in, and dislocation of, their communicative activity (arguably one of the most significant categories of social life in modern societies) while those not so well placed remain 'locals' whose prospects, while certainly more rooted, are experienced as more limited by most contemporary stan-dards (Luke 1998: 129–34). Put simply, in the network society place matters insofar as it either enables or disables computer-mediated escape from the constraints place or loca-tion enforce upon communication.

These considerations are part of a broader discussion of the role played by new information and communication tech-nologies in the dynamics of globalization, at least one aspect of which involves a perceived collapse of local (with 'local' typically, and problematically, identified with 'national') dis-tinctions in economic, cultural and political practices. In this respect, digital networks share in the universalist essence of technology. It is possible to isolate several concrete symptoms of this condition: the consolidation and proliferation of Western mass culture (Hannigan 2002); the global harmonization of public policy in communication sectors (McChesney 1999; Raboy 2002; D. Schiller 1999); declines in locally defined civic and community identification (Putnam 2000); and standardization of management, work and labour practices, especially in low-skill occupations that involve a high degree of computer mediation (Menzies 1996; Rochlin 1997). To be sure, none of these phenomena can be attributed totally to the essence of technology; countless variable factors of design, situation and application or use have also contributed to these outcomes. Nevertheless, it would not be unreasonable to suggest that these practices are at least consistent with aspects of technological mediation identified by substantivist critics as essential to technology more generally, and so can be understood as instances in which the essence of technology has been made concrete.

Design of network technology

Thinking through the essence of technology can reveal a great deal to us about our specific encounter with digital networks, but it would be unreasonable to suggest that the essence of technology determines outright the comprehensive character of this technology's outcome in the world, or that the substantivist framework tells us everything we might need to know about it. As such, we must also look to other considerations, including the actual design of these instruments and the technicality of their application. Such consideration is crucial precisely because, contrary to the assumption of instrumentalism, the design of technological instruments is never neutral. 'Technical things', as Langdon Winner has put it, 'have political qualities', and not all of these can be attributed to the social and political conditions in which the technology is situated (Winner 1986: 19).

According to Winner, technological artefacts can be said to 'have politics' in two distinct, but related, senses. In the first instance, 'the invention, design, or arrangement of a specific device or technical system becomes a way of settling an issue in the affairs of a particular community' (Winner 1986: 22). As an example, Winner points to highway over-passes on New York's Long Island, deliberately designed by Robert Moses so as to be too low to allow passage beneath them by public buses. This design decision was also a political decision, and the technical arrangement it put in place was also a political arrangement that settled an unsettling issue: low overpasses effectively denied poor people and racial minorities (people who customarily could not afford automobiles and instead used public transport) access to the public park and beaches to which the parkways led. In this case, a political outcome that might be difficult to achieve legislatively could be easily accomplished technologically, through delegation to a technical artefact or device. It is to this quality that Feenberg alludes when he points out the legislative character of technological design:

> The masters of technical systems, corporate and military leaders, physicians and engineers, have far more control over patterns of urban growth, the design of dwellings and trans-portation systems, the selection of innovations, our experience as employees, patients and consumers, than all the electoral institutions of our society put together. The technical codes that shape our lives reflect particular social interests to which we have delegated the power to decide where and how we live, what kinds of food we eat, how we communicate, are entertained, healed and so on. (Feenberg 1999: 131)

Indeed, it is arguable that the tendency for technological designs to constitute political arrangements is most pro-nounced in the area of communication, a human practice that is indispensable to, and often definitive of, political life more generally. At least since Marshall McLuhan uttered the famous aphorism, 'the medium is the message', and observed that 'the content of a medium is like the juicy piece of meat carried by the burglar to distract the watchdog of the mind', communication theorists have understood that the design of communications media often has a greater effect upon social structure and practice than the substance of that which is transmitted via those instruments (McLuhan 1964: 32).

It is precisely this sensibility that American legal scholar Lawrence Lessig has brought to his influential study of the *architecture* and basic *design* of the internet. 'Architecture', writes Lessig, 'is a kind of law: it determines what people can and cannot do' (Lessig 1999: 59). In terms of the internet, architecture is constructed through the 'code' embedded in the software and hardware devices that together comprise this technology. As Lessig puts it: 'In cyberspace, we must understand how code regulates – how the software and hardware that make cyberspace what it is *regulate* cyberspace as it is . . . *Code is law*' (Lessig 1999: 6). As law, choices about code – i.e., choices about the fundamental design of the medium – are necessarily *political* choices: 'We can build, or architect, or code cyberspace to protect values that we believe are fundamental, or we can build, or architect, or code cyberspace to allow those values to disappear. There is no middle ground' (Lessig 1999: 6). In Lessig's view, the crucial design choice for the internet is whether its architecture will be coded to support the anonymity or identification of its users and their activities: the former will encourage privacy and liberty; the latter will enable surveillance and regulation, and is the option favoured by commercial interests hoping to exploit the medium as an exchange market in which contractual obligations to buy and sell can be secured and enforced. It is also increasingly the option favoured by governments sensitive to the security liabilities posed by a medium of communication that makes it difficult to identify and locate parties using the medium to organize, or even carry out, criminal activity. Whatever the outcome, it is clear that such design choices are more than just 'a question of engineering', and are, in fact, 'choices about how the world will be ordered, and about which values will be given precedence' (Lessig 1999: 59). From this perspective, technical design takes on a heightened and perhaps unique importance in human affairs.

In a second sense, technological designs are sometimes understood as 'inherently political' insofar as they 'appear to require or to be strongly compatible with particular kinds of political relationships' (Winner 1986: 22). Here, technological devices and systems are not as flexible, or open to alternative social and political consequences, as Lessig's account of the choices we have to make regarding the internet's fundamental code would suggest. In Lessig's account, the code or design of the internet will constitute a particular political order, constraining some practices and enabling others, but, as a technology, the internet is still open to a choice between one design, and one set of social consequences, and another. An inherently political technology, by contrast, 'unavoidably brings with it conditions for human relationships that have a distinctive political cast – for example, centralized or decentralized, egalitarian or inegalitarian, repressive or liberating' (Winner 1986: 29). Complex technical systems with high stakes are, in this view, fundamentally incompatible with democracy and make strict, centralized control by elites a practical necessity: absent chains of expert command, large-scale systems are liable to collapse. A contemporary example of a technology often presented as inherently political is nuclear weapons, whose presence in our midst practically necessitates highly centralized forms of political authority capable of controlling the distribution of these weapons: absent reliable, centralized authority, global annihilation would result.

Of course, this conceptualization of some technologies as 'inherently political' strays into the territory of technological determinism. As Winner points out, it is possible to construct a less deterministic version of the argument, a version that says some technologies are 'strongly compatible with, but do not strictly require, social and political relationships of a particular stripe' (Winner 1986: 32). There has certainly been no shortage of claims of this kind with regard to the internet. Popular discourse surrounding digital information and communication technologies – particularly in the early days of their development – widely supposed, for example, that the decentralized, territorially indefinite architecture of the internet rendered it *in*compatible with the sort of centralized legal and regulatory authority traditionally exercised by sovereign nation-states, and more compatible with self-organizing, market-based, anarchic political arrangements. While not completely without foundation, this prospect must be tempered by the reality that these technologies appear to be every bit as compatible with centralized regulation as they are with self-organizing, grassroots democracy (Kalathil and Boas

2003). As mentioned above, a considerable body of analysis suggests the re-establishment of centralized control amidst the complexity of late industrial society was the primary motivating factor in the development and deployment of advanced information and communication technologies in the latter half of the twentieth century. In this view, the information or network revolution is best described as a 'control revolution' (Beniger 1986). Still, others, such as Andrew Shapiro, maintain that the rise of network technology indeed does represent a 'control revolution', but one in which these instruments mediate 'a potentially momentous transfer of power from large institutions to individuals . . . Hierarchies are coming undone. Gatekeepers are being bypassed. Power is devolving to "end users" ' (Shapiro 1999: 10–11). The word 'potentially' is key here. As Shapiro points out, the political outcome of this technology will still depend on the ongoing contests over its design and configuration. As he puts it: 'code may be at the heart of various power struggles in the digital age' (Shapiro 1999: 15). It is perhaps necessary to invert this observation as well: various power struggles over code will, at least partially, determine the character of the digital age.

So, the design of network technology clearly matters, but its contested nature suggests that the internet is not an example of an 'inherently political technology' in the sense articulated by Winner, given the lingering contingency regarding the sorts of political arrangements it is likely to mediate, and the political principles that might inform its deployment. Much will depend on the priorities and interests animating the actors and institutions controlling the medium's development. Inherently political technologies are, it should be conceded, quite rare, but this should not detract from our appreciation of the political stakes in technological design. Whether their politics are inherent or not, technologies such as the internet are inextricably 'central features in widely shared arrangements and conditions of life in contemporary society', and issues pertaining to their design necessarily 'concern how the members of society manage their common affairs and seek the common good' (Winner 1995: 67). The design of network technology is thus crucial to the broader outcomes of these technologies in the world.

Situation of network technology

A third element at play in the determination of technological outcome is *situation*, which is meant to gather the various social, political and economic aspects of the *contexts* in which technologies and their use are situated. Not everything significant in a technological outcome is given by a technology's essence and design – a great deal is socially constructed. As suggested by the social constructivist perspective, technologies do not develop, and they are not used, in a vacuum. Instead, technological outcomes necessarily have a historical and sociological character. They are developed and used in the context of pre-existing social, political and economic relationships, networks of actors, and conditions that enforce various priorities and norms on the technology and its elaboration in practice. Just as new technologies give something to social, political and economic life, so too do the conditions of social, political and economic life lend something to the actual outcome of technological change. Castells, for example, suggests that the development of digital technologies was not, on its own, sufficient to produce what he has described as the network society. These technologies have had a transformative effect, he argues, only because they are situated in the context of particular socio-historical conditions, namely, 'the needs of the economy for management flexibility and for the globalization of capital, production and trade; [and] the demands of society in which the values of individual freedom and open communication become paramount' (Castells 2001: 2). It is, according to Castells, the complementarity of these technologies and these contextual factors that produces the outcome that is 'a new social structure predominantly based on networks' (Castells 2001: 2).

Even below the level of a potential societal transformation, it is necessary to pay attention to the importance of a technology's situation. Like design, conditions in the social, political and economic environment in which a technology is situated both enable and disable certain outcomes. Phrased another way, we could say that under certain situational conditions, technological deployments lead to particular outcomes that might not arise under other situational conditions.

Similarly, we can say that certain situational conditions can undermine the potential of alternative deployments and uses of the same technology. This can be illustrated in a number of ways. For example, the outcome of digital networks in a polity that enforces strong privacy legislation will differ from the outcome of this same technology in a polity where such protections are weak or unenforced. The outcome of the internet in a society based on grossly unequal distributions of material security, resources and power will be quite different than the outcome of the internet in a more egalitarian society. The outcome of network-mediated communication will differ greatly between social contexts in which gender discrimination is widespread and those in which it is less prevalent. When we consider that the situation of a technology actually involves multiple, overlapping contexts that are also dynamic and change over time (not to mention the fact that situations change once the technology itself *becomes* part of the context in which it is situated), we begin to appreciate the complex relationship between situation and technological outcomes.

Situation, or context, also factors into the determination of the design choices that determine the technical configuration of technological instruments. The choices that are made about design are made on the basis of the values held by those empowered to make those choices. Relationships of power, and social priorities, derived from a technology's situation are thus, in a sense, *designed into* instruments. And so questions about who is empowered to make choices about design, about what they value or fear, and about how their particular advantages and disadvantages are affected by particular design or deployment choices, are crucial to technological outcomes. It is here that the politics of technology begins to reveal itself.

A good example of the political effect of situation upon the design of network technology is provided by Lessig, who points out that the code of the early architecture of the internet was biased against regulation and towards openness, against the identification of users and labelling of their activity and towards anonymity and liberty, towards access and away from control (Lessig 1999: 30–42). This was because in the context of the medium's development – a context in which it was conceived primarily as a tool of academic research and resource sharing – those who controlled and made decisions about its early design valued openness, publicity, accessibility and liberty.

However, as Lessig argues, whereas the code of the early internet was biased towards *unregulability*, that code is in the process of flipping, and becoming a code of *regulability* and control. Why? Because the context in which the decisions about the design of the medium are being carried out has changed dramatically. The design of the internet is changing because the internet's *situation* is changing. One aspect of this change is that the medium is now developing in a context in which the exploitation of its *commercial* potential is becoming an overriding value. Commerce is impossible without regulation – a medium that escapes regulation cannot be a medium of commerce. Commerce requires that transactions be secured, that contractual obligations be met, that promises be kept, that property be protected – all of which requires enforcement, which in turn rests upon reliable identification of parties to transactions, and verification of their activities. A certain degree of regulation, of one kind or another, and commerce go together. And as Lessig points out, once the commercial potential of exchanging data in various forms via computer networks was identified and seized upon by powerful commercial interests, an architecture of control or regulation became a priority. As he puts it, 'For e-commerce to develop fully, the Net will need a far more general architecture of trust – an architecture that makes possible secure and private transactions' (Lessig 1999: 40). This architecture rests on building protocols of authentication, authorization and identification, and means of surveillance, into network functioning as a condition of access and use.

Not incidentally, this architecture also responds to another new element of the situation in which networks are developing. Here I refer to the heightened value placed on security, and the perception that unregulated communication networks like the internet can be a threat to security when they are either used as a tool by actors whose intentions are to do harm, or as a target for their disruptive and harmful tactics. The increasing worry that an unregulated internet is both a tool and a target for terrorists is a crucial part of the environment in which this technology is situated, and it enforces certain priorities upon its design and deployment. Fears of an anarchic communication medium have been present since the onset of network technology (expressed at an early juncture in relation to online pornography and sexual predation). These fears persist, though their purchase has escalated in the aftermath of the attacks in 2001 on the United States, and the emergence of evidence that the internet was used in the planning of those attacks (Thomas 2003). The response, in the United States and elsewhere, has been legislation that not only authorizes increased levels of state surveillance of digitally mediated communication, but also requires technology companies and access providers to make such surveillance easier to carry out (Rotenberg 2002).

Thus, the priorities of commerce and security have combined to create a situation that is pushing the outcome of network technology in a particular direction. The possibility exists that a different situation – different values, different priorities, different people with different interests empowered to make decisions – could contribute to different outcomes. It is also the case that establishing the parameters of a technology's situation is somewhat arbitrary, and almost necessarily incomplete. The contexts in which network technology is situated are multiple, diverse and complex. An analysis of this technology's outcome will be unable to capture all of these; nevertheless, it must at least seek to be sensitive to both the importance of situation, and its irreducible complexity.

Uses of network technology

The final element involved in determining the character of a technological outcome is *use*. A substantial portion of the social effect of a given technology can be accounted for by the manner in which the technology is actually used by individuals and groups in concrete social situations. Indeed, it is possible to argue that use patterns are the primary determinant of technological outcomes – that rather than the essence, design or situation of a technology, it is the character of a technology's everyday and extraordinary uses that determines its ultimate, lasting impact. In this view, part of the social construction of technological outcomes is the choices people make and the practices they develop as users of technological instruments.

In many cases, uses are prescribed, standardized and adopted by individuals who assume the posture of consumers in choosing either to use the technology in the manner prescribed, or not to use it at all. Arguably, this is the manner in which most everyday users encounter technology. In these cases, use is still a significant variable in the technological outcome, insofar as it confirms and does not challenge the intended dispensation given in the technology's essence, design and situation. In other cases, however, users intervene and appropriate the technology for purposes other than those prescribed. In these cases, use is still *conditioned* by some concoction of essence, design and situation – use always has to be *allowed for* by these other variables, but it does not have to be *intended*. You can't use a technology in a manner that its design disallows (you *can't* catch a cod with a lighthouse); however, you can use technologies in ways that their designers might not have intended, but which their designs nevertheless allow (you *can* use a lighthouse as a museum). We appropriate technologies for uses other than those for which they were designed all the time. The development of the communication utility of networked computers is itself an example of this sort of appropriation for unintended use. Initially, digital networks were designed and constructed to enable remote time-share access to the computing power of large, mainframe computers. However, as connectivity proliferated, this prescribed use was quickly eclipsed as users appropriated the technology as a communication medium (i.e., for e-mail), a use that was not only unprescribed but also largely unauthorized in the early days of networks (Abbate 2000: 106–11).

People use technologies in many ways, some of which are given to them, and some of which are unintended by design and undetermined by situation. In some cases, user choices and use patterns simply reflect existing structures and relationships of power; in other cases, they undermine them. There is, it would seem, a substantial range of possibilities between what Lewis Mumford identified decades ago as the poles of 'authoritarian and democratic technics' (Mumford

1964: 1). Feenberg has characterized uses that tend towards the latter pole as species of 'democratic rationalization', by which he means to indicate creative uses that challenge or subvert existing hierarchies of power and control embedded in a technology, and which employ the technology to serve needs or principles that are unmet or ignored by its pre-scribed, intended applications (Feenberg 1999: 76). As an example, Feenberg cites the user-driven transformation of France's Minitel videotext system from one designed to provide public access to databases to one used for interpersonal communication. Indeed, it would seem that subversive rationalization at least equals intention and design when it comes to the manner in which network technology has unfolded, and continues to unfold, into everyday application. It is perhaps for this reason that Castells identifies the hacker ethic – arguably responsible for two of the most significant emerging applications of network technology, the open-source software movement (e.g., Linux) and peer-to-peer file swapping (e.g., Napster) – as central to the cultural dimensions of the network society (Castells 2001: 41–52).

Consideration of application or use is clearly indispensable to reckoning with the outcome of any technology. However, it is not so clear exactly how this consideration can or should be carried out, especially in the context of a technology, such as digital networks, whose uses are multiple, proliferating and evolving. It is not easy to answer the question 'How, or for what purposes, are digital information and communication technologies used?' Several studies, both globally and in specific national and regional contexts, have concentrated, for example, on trying to describe the characteristics of everyday internet use (Wellman and Haythornethwaite 2002). Thus, we have learned that, in North America, e-mail among friends, family and colleagues ranks highest among everyday uses of the internet. Web-browsing ranks second, with searches for product, service and hobby information (including entertainment and sports information) typically ranking highest among browsing activities (Howard et al. 2002; United States Department of Commerce 2002). Typically, new users tend to more instrumental uses (i.e., searching for specific information related to some offline end), while experienced users exhibit increased recreational use of the medium (i.e., as a social end in itself). The authors of a global study of use patterns assert, 'Experience and [recent] data suggest that internet use worldwide will follow the North American developmental path' (Chen et al. 2002: 109).

However, it is not at all clear whether personal internet use is the most important category of use when it comes to networked, digital information and communication technologies. Perhaps mobile telephony is equally significant. It is also not clear that the personal uses that individuals make of e-mail and the web is as central to the social outcome of digital technologies as the myriad other uses to which these technologies are put, in a vast variety of forms and contexts. It is arguable that the use of digital computer networks and databases by national and international security authorities is a more significant application of these technologies, in terms of their social outcome, than their use by private individuals to send e-mail to their friends or to engage in role-playing games. Similarly, it is arguable that the penetration of network technologies into workplaces, sites of production, the infrastructure of global commerce and the practice of warfare – in a phrase, their use as *technologies of systems control* – will ultimately be more important to the shape of the network society than their use as technologies of interpersonal and mass communication. In any case, how do we venture an approximation of the uses of network technology that would not require volumes to express? And how do we do it in the midst of a technology whose development is as yet unfinished? The question about the role of use in technological outcomes, so imperative to ask, is nearly impossible to answer, at least comprehensively or definitively. This, of course, does not relieve us of the need to ask it.

From network technology to network society

The complex relationship of essence, design, situation and use that ultimately produces technological outcomes suggests that the basic technical attributes of a given instrument are only one part of what ultimately becomes of a technology in the world. That being said, several contemporary writers have attempted to articulate, in broad strokes, the characteristic outcomes of digital network technologies. To close this chapter, it might be useful to consider some of the ways in which technological qualities of digital information and communication networks have been linked with fundamentally new conditions for human sociability typically associated with the 'network society'.

Time–space compression

One of the most often repeated observations about new media technologies is that they are media of *time–space compression*. What does this mean? It means that they work on our experience of space and time, specifically that they make physical distance and the passage of time seem shorter, or more compressed, at least insofar as activities involving communication are concerned. In his book *The Condition of Postmodernity*, David Harvey defined 'time–space compression' as

> processes that so revolutionize the objective qualities of space and time that we are forced to alter, sometimes in quite radical ways, how we represent the world to ourselves. I use the word 'compression' because a strong case can be made that the history of capitalism has been characterized by speed-up in the pace of life, while so overcoming spatial barriers that the world sometimes seems to collapse inward upon us. (Harvey 1989: 240)

In Harvey's view, intensification of the dynamic of time–space compression is the distinctive mark of postmodernity. In the age of network technology, we have grown very accustomed to hearing suggestions that the world has become smaller (i.e., 'the global village') and that everything happens faster as a result of the proliferation of new media. Essentially, this is a result of the facility of digital communication networks for mediating the communication or flow of vast quantities of digital information across great physical distances at truly remarkable speeds.

If there is a consensus among those who reflect upon the social implications of digital media, it is that these technologies – despite whatever else they do – operate on our experience of space and time. In the network society, social, political and economic attention and activity are increasingly concentrated upon, and mediated by, flows of data that race across vast distances in an instant. Under these conditions, location or placement in time remain salient primarily to those unfortunates lacking adequate network connectivity. Within the grasp of connectivity, however, 'Localities become disembodied from their cultural, historical, geographic meaning . . . inducing a space of flows that substitutes for the space of places. Time is erased in the new communication system . . . The space of flows and timeless time are the material foundations of a new culture . . . the culture of real virtuality' (Castells 1996: 375). In this configuration of human experience, places exist primarily as points of origin and destination for flows, time is rendered into timelessness, and location is dissolved, at least for those whose access to network technologies qualifies them for membership into the network society.

Deterritorialization

Related to this dynamic of time–space compression is another attribute typically associated with new media: their purportedly global or deterritorialized nature. Previous media of communication – the telegraph and telephone, for example, not to mention the letter sent by post – have enabled communication across the globe, but never has there been a communication technology that has enabled, with such ease, at such relatively modest expense, in such volumes, at such great speeds, and with such reliability, complex yet routine communication between multiple parties scattered almost all over the globe. Never has there been a mass communication system that seems *so little* contained or constrained by territorial expanse.

Another way to put this is that, in network societies, new communication technologies reconfigure the conceptual and material relationship between communication and geography, in which distance ceases to a determining factor. That being said, it would be a mistake to equate network-mediated deterritorialization in this sense, with an end of geography as such. In his more recent writing, Castells appears sensitive to the implications of claims that the network society is without geography, a society of placelessness. Here, he writes,

> In fact, the Internet has a geography of its own, a geography made of networks and nodes that process information flows generated and managed from places ... The resulting space of flows is a new form of space, characteristic of the Information Age, but it is not placeless: it links places by telecommunicated computer networks and computerized transportation systems. It redefines distance but does not cancel geography. (Castells 2001: 207)

In one sense, this passage reflects a contemporary discursive tendency to deploy terms like 'space' or 'place' metaphorically, or at least in a manner that redefines these concepts such that they no longer refer to the physical things we associate with them in plain language. It is this redefinition that makes it possible, in network society discourse, to refer to a simulated environment in cyber*space* as a *place*. In another sense, however, Castells's identification of the 'geography of the Internet' serves to remind us that despite the fact that an increasing volume of human communication is now mediated primarily or exclusively via digital networks, the fact remains that the material world outside these networks of communication persists, and that its stubborn reality cannot be denied. It is the stubborn materiality of the world, for example, that accounts for the highly differential rates of network development, access and use throughout the world, the so-called 'digital divide' (Norris 2001). When the majority of the population in the affluent world has internet access at home, while similar majorities in the poorest regions lack access to plain old telephone service, claims about the irrelevance of geography become difficult to sustain, and assume a distinctly ideological flavour. Networks may deterritorialize communication for those who enjoy access to them, but they do not eliminate the material reality of the world in which those networks and the communication they mediate are situated.

Nevertheless, the deterritorializing operation of digital communication networks is thought to contribute to several contemporary social-economic and political dynamics. Among these are the organization and coordination of economic activity on a global scale – the globalization of production, finance and trade; the global consumption of (largely American) cultural and entertainment commodities; the difficulties facing territorially organized political power (i.e., nation-states) in regulating and policing activities mediated by these technologies; the organization and mobilization of non-territorially defined social and political movements and groupings (including, ironically, the anti-globalization movement). These dynamics are real, not virtual, and they extend, at least in part, from the complex relationship between network technologies that serve to deterritorialize communication, and a world where geography continues to matter.

Decentralization and control

Another attribute typically associated with new media technologies and the societies they mediate is decentralization. Because they are based on a distributed architecture, network media enable a wide array of communicative practices – content generation, message transmission – that do not originate from, and are not effectively controlled or regulated by, a single central source or agent. Network technologies have made possible the phenomenon of a highly *decentralized* but still *mass* communication medium. We can distinguish new media from old media like the broadcast technologies in this respect. Radio and television are broadcast technologies, which means that they communicate information transmitted from a central source to a multitude of dispersed receivers simultaneously. The exclusivity of access to the complex production and distribution technology necessary for radio and television broadcasting, and the limitations of the spectrum for transmitting information in this way, mean that the vast majority of people participate in these forms of communication only as audience members – as receivers but not producers of content. This produces a communication system in which the power to communicate is relatively concentrated, and quite centralized.

Digital networks – due to their distributed architecture and the relative accessibility of highly sophisticated and powerful computing devices and programmes – are a more decentralized medium. Here, the technology of reception is the same as the technology of production – anyone who has the technology to receive communication via a computer network also has the technology to produce the content of communication. What's more, they have ready access to a relatively cheap but also extremely widespread and efficient system of mass distribution in the network itself, a system in which there are multiple points of entry into, and navigation around, the network, rather than tightly controlled (and easily regulated) centralized access. This does not mean that all those with network access have equal power as sources of information: CNN remains more powerful than I am, despite the fact that we can both post material on the internet. Regardless of this fact (more evidence of the stubborn persistence of the material reality of the world outside the network), it is the set of attributes outlined above that often leads to descriptions of network societies as those in which hierarchies supported by centralized communication media have become difficult to sustain.

This latter characterization is especially interesting, given that this attribute of decentralization has an unlikely twin, and that twin is centralized control. While it is true that the decentralized attributes of digital communication networks make it a challenge to exert centralized control over the medium itself, it is also the case that the technical properties of digital networks set up very well as technologies of systems control.

In order to operate 'under control' (i.e., directed purposively to pre-determined ends) complex systems (like an army, a courier system, a global airline reservation system, a global system of production or finance) require the communication, gathering and processing of a great deal of information in a short period of time, in order that activities within the system can be coordinated, directed and adjusted in response to changing conditions. The technicalities of digital computer networks are perhaps uniquely suited to these demands, and so they have emerged as having considerable utility as technologies of systems control – despite the fact that the decentralized character of new media technologies themselves means that they are somewhat resistant to the centralized control that characterized, for example, broadcast technologies (Rochlin 1997). The recent history of online pornography, denial of service attacks against major corporate websites, and the proliferation of peer-to-peer file swapping speaks to the difficulty of exerting centralized control over decentralized network media. Yet, it is also true that digital technologies are indispensable to the control of the complex transnational enterprises that dominate the global economy, as well as to escalating and proliferating regimes of private and state surveillance. Various writers have isolated one or the other of these attributes as definitive of this technology, often depending upon whether they see in it a promise or peril for individual liberty and democracy. Typically, this taking of sides also entails a conviction that one of these dynamics will eliminate the possibility of the other, as the future of these technologies unfolds. This may happen, but it is also possible that the dialectic of decentralization and control will be a permanent, constitutive element of any society where use of these technologies is widespread.

Interactivity and customization

A fourth attribute typically associated with the social impact of digital network technology is its capacity to mediate interactive communications. By definition, all human communication involves interaction between people. To the extent it enables widespread human communication, network technology is thus highly interactive in this respect. This is the sort of interactivity that people refer to in relation to the dialogic applications of the internet – e-mail, discussion lists, chat rooms, multiple-user domains, online gaming, etc.

However, when new media are described as highly interactive, something beyond these dialogic applications is signalled. Typically the term interactivity also refers to the capacity of digital communications media to enable a high degree of intervention and choice by users concerning the manner in which they receive information. This interactive quality of new media is contrasted with the highly non-interactive character of previous mass media forms such as radio and television broadcasting and mass print publication – wherein receivers of information basically get what they are offered in the form in which it is offered – that is to say, under these previous forms, the reception of communicated information was highly passive. Network communication, by contrast, is at least potentially very interactive, enabling a higher degree of discretion and intervention on the part of receivers of information. Perhaps the most prominent example of this sort of interactivity is hypertext – the coding of world wide web pages that enables users to navigate through, across and between documents at their discretion, in ways not always intended by the publishers of that information. The case with which digitized material can be copied, stored, reorganized, duplicated and redistributed is another manifestation of interactivity.

In sum, the interactive attributes of digital networks contribute to a medium that makes possible a highly customized and personalized mass communication experience – which seems like an oxymoron, a contradiction of the very notion of mass communication, which is associated with standardization, rigidity, homogeneity and predictability. Indeed, a phrase has arisen to capture this seemingly contradictory aspect of network technology: mass customization. This attribute is thought to have implications for a wide array of social, economic and political practices. In some cases, customization and personalization are characterized as conducive to individual empowerment and an erosion of the power of centralized communication institutions and information distributors. It is this quality that gives rise to the notion that the network society is one in which individuals – citizens, consumers, working people – are increasingly in charge. On the other hand, it is also argued that the customization enabled by network technology is largely superficial, that interactive choices serve primarily to add to the storehouses of data that enable increasingly sophisticated techniques of surveillance and control, and that personalization supports the privatization and fragmentation of things like community, the public sphere, and various other sources of social solidarity. Whether conceived in positive or negative terms, it is certain that notions of customization and personalization are central to the imagination of the network society.

This chapter has covered considerable ground. It began by reviewing contending theoretical approaches to the question of technology – instrumentalism, substantivism, social constructivism – and recommended a composite approach adopting the insights of each of these perspectives. This composite approach involved consideration of the several factors that contribute to technological outcomes in the world: the essence of technology, design, situation and use. Each of these was then explored in reference to the particular instance of digital network technologies. To conclude, a number of socially significant attributes of the operation of network technology were considered, including time–space compression, deterritorialization, decentralization and control, and interactivity and customization. The chapters that follow will consider in greater detail how some of these attributes come to bear in the economic, political and social outcomes of network technology.

3
Network Economy

To the extent it exists as a discernible historical formation, the network society is an outgrowth of the operation of capitalist economies under the auspices of digital technologies. This is to say, despite the rhetoric of revolution that typically accompanies moments of significant technological innovation, and which certainly has captured a great deal of the public imagination in relation to the spread of new information and communication technologies, the network society is a species of capitalism. In this sense, its development represents a deep continuity, rather than a fundamental rupture, in the economic trajectory of modern Western society. This is not to say that nothing is changing in terms of the organization and operation of capitalist economies in response to the possibilities thrown up by the new technologies. Things are definitely changing. However, whether we choose to designate these organizational and operational changes 'revolutionary' depends entirely on how we decide to define that word. To be sure, even Karl Marx, whose hopes rested on the revolution that would eliminate capitalism, recognized that a certain kind of change – 'constant revolutionizing of the means of production' – was, in fact, definitive of advanced industrial economies, and clearly in the interests of the established order (Marx and Engels 1986: 37). But these changes take place squarely within the continued near-ubiquity of the capitalist mode of production, and so it is important to be careful about the terms we use to describe them. It is perhaps only in the context of a society in which a new design for sneakers can be called revolutionary that we would also happily use that word to name a technological change that, for example, greatly enhances the ability of employers to exercise comprehensive surveillance over the performance and behaviour of their employees, or that provides a new medium for the extension of consumer culture.

Thus, as Castells describes it, the rise of the network society is 'linked to the *expansion* and *rejuvenation* of capitalism, as industrialism was linked to its constitution as a mode of production' (Castells 1996: 19; emphasis added). For Castells, the logic and technologies of networks were central to the restructuring of global capitalism in the 1980s and 1990s, on a model that he labels 'informationalism'. Here, Castells means to suggest a process whereby the industrial model of capitalism has been infiltrated extensively by the ganglia of digital networks. As he puts it, 'while the informational/global economy is distinct from the industrial economy, it does not oppose its logic. It subsumes it through technological deepening, embodying knowledge and information in all processes of material production and distribution . . . In other words, the industrial economy had to become informational and global or collapse' (Castells 1996: 91–2). Whether 'informational capitalism' has comprehensively replaced its industrial forebear remains a matter of considerable debate. Industrial forms and practices certainly persist, even in societies highly penetrated by new information technologies. The point, however, is that even if 'informationalism' is a new species of capitalism, the fact remains that it is still *a species of capitalism*, rather than a wholly novel economic system.

As Christopher May has recently written, 'while we may be living through a period in which the form and practices of our lives are changing in many ways, the underlying substance of our socioeconomic system remains largely the same' (May 2002: 1). The distinction here between change at the level of *form* and *practice*, and continuity at the level of *substance* is key. Perhaps then, a shift from industrial to informational capitalism is a significant change in form; and perhaps the change from strictly hierarchical to decentralized operations and management is an important change in practice. These changes, however, must be situated within an appreciation of certain basic continuities in the substance of capitalism, to which these same technologies also make a significant contribution. These include, for example, private property; commodification; class relations; free markets; massive public and private systems for the stimulation and management of consumption; accumulation as a central strategic motivation, etc. Consequently, below the brilliant surface of re-engineered economic organization and process, 'our lives', as May observes, 'in many ways remain relatively unchanged' (May 2002: 2).

Capitalism, then, is the major element of the context in which the development of network technology, and the society it mediates, is situated. Network technology, and the network society, reflect and confirm the dynamics and parameters of life under a capitalist economy. Still, recalling the perspective presented in chapter 2, it would be unwise to deny that these technologies, in their design, deployment and use, have had a tremendous impact upon those dynamics and parameters. This chapter will consider those aspects of the relationship between network technologies and contemporary capitalism that have emerged as central to the network society thesis. These include capitalist globalization; the rise of the so-called 'new economy'; network enterprises; non-standard forms of work and employment; and the status of property. From this survey, a portrait of the capitalism of the network society should emerge.

Networks and globalization

As suggested in chapter 1, the economic organization of the network society cannot be separated from the dynamics of economic globalization that have characterized the latter decades of the twentieth century. In broad terms, economic globalization refers to the transnational organization of capitalist firms, production, finance, services, trade, investment and markets, made possible in part by a variety of international economic agreements in which constituent nation-states have agreed to relax nationally specific controls on a wide range of economic activities. Globalization thus names not only the organization of the capitalist economy across national political borders, but also the constitution of that economy on a neo-liberal model – in which market actors are increasing free of regulatory constraint and states find their interventionist and redistributive options increasingly hedged – whose adoption has reached near-universal levels.

The development and proliferation of network technology and the dynamics of economic globalization are intimately linked. As Ronald Deibert has detailed, there is a definite historical 'fitness' between what he describes as the 'hypermedia environment' and the shift from a modern, nationally organized political and economic order to a postmodern, globally organized one (Deibert 1997: 137). This fitness manifests itself in number of ways.

First, these technologies are instrumental to the operation of the global economy, providing an infrastructure and control technology for the execution and coordination of economic activities (i.e., production, consumption, trade, finance) that are territorially disaggregated and dynamic. For example, coordination of complex systems of transnational production would be impossible on the scale such systems now exist without the particular utilities of networked communication technologies. Specifically, the utility of these technologies for communicating huge volumes of complex data across vast distances instantaneously and automatically enables the remote control and coordination of decentralized production, supply and distribution systems. Without effective, efficient telecommunications, global enterprises would simply lack the agility, responsiveness and flexibility necessary to execute operations profitably on such a gross scale. As we will discuss further below, network technologies make possible the multi-firm collaborative ventures and flexible, just-in-time production processes that also characterize the global production environment. As Deibert describes, 'electronic connections link companies from all parts of the production chain both domestically and internationally into a rapid response/mutual adjustment system that often begins the moment the bar code is scanned at the retail register when the product is purchased' (Deibert 1997: 143).

These technologies are similarly indispensable to the operation of the global system of finance and capital circulation. Indeed, the relationship here is perhaps best described as one of reciprocity, in which information and communication technologies and the globalization of finance and capital feed off and drive each other. Deibert's description of this reciprocity is evocative:

> pressures in the direction of financial globalization created a demand for, and spurred on new developments in, communication technologies, while the latter, in turn, fuelled the globalization processes of the former. Without hypermedia, the global financial structure could not exist on so formidable a scale as it does today ... Like the tightening of a knot, each advanced application of hypermedia in the financial sector furthers and deepens the global integration of capital markets in a planetary web of complex speculative financial flows. (Deibert 1997: 148, 152)

It is also the case that digital communication technologies are central to the production and circulation of the branded entertainment and information commodities that increasingly drive the consumer end of the global economy, and contribute to the maintenance of a global commercial culture that operates notwithstanding national particularities. Network technologies are the delivery system for 'a universal particular that is favoured by globalized capital, electronic means of production, and uniform mass culture' (Hannigan 2002: 21). It is possible to exaggerate the degree of cultural homogenization that prevails in the context of globalization, and it is important to recognize the extent to which the forces of global commercial culture have been compelled, and able, to adjust to enduring local peculiarities of taste and market (Deibert 1997: 144–5). Still, this qualification does not detract from the central point here: digital networks and their ancillary technologies play an indispensable role as the medium, infrastructure or circulatory system of economic processes – in this case the consumption of cultural commodities – organized and executed on a global scale.

The globalization of the capitalist economy on the model of market liberalism also sets the conditions under which network telecommunication technologies have been developed and deployed. The characteristics of the global economy – the constrained political and economic autonomy of sovereign nation-states; the limitations imposed by international trade and investment agreements and the international institutions that enforce them; the contraction of the redistributive and regulatory functions of nation-states; the remarkable concentration of economic power in the hands of a decreasing number of horizontally and vertically integrated transnational corporations – these are the political-economic conditions under which the design and use of network technologies and their applications will continue to unfold. As discussed above, network technologies have been a crucial enabler of the globalization of the capitalist economy; they are also subject to, and situated within, the limitations and direction imposed by that economy.

This situation has come to bear in a number of ways, most of which arise from the integration of telecommunication and media sectors into the regime of global neo-liberalism that has prevailed since the 1980s. This economic regime is characterized by four primary orientations: the privatization of public enterprises; the liberalization of markets; a reorientation of the goal of state regulation away from securing the public interest against market failure and towards creating a hospitable climate for investment and enterprise; and the commercialization/corporatization of the public sector (Murdock and Golding 2001: 114). The institutionalization of this neo-liberal framework in the global media and telecom sectors comprises a complex and detailed history, but its primary contours are easily sketched (see McChesney 1999; Raboy 2002; D. Schiller 1999). In the 1980s, fresh from their withdrawal from Unesco in protest over the MacBride Commission's call for a 'New World Information and Communication Order' that would staunch the unequal flow of information and cultural products from the wealthy North to the less affluent South, governments in the United States and the United Kingdom began to develop an alternative vision of the role of communication in the emerging global economy. In this vision, mass communication – both its content and its media – would become a key driver of economic growth and the global activity of transnational corporations. This would require liberalization of the market conditions under which private firms could develop and exploit the potential of new information technologies, services and commodities, and a commitment to build a communication infrastructure configured to support these activities without subjecting them to undue regulatory constraint.

This process began on a national level in the United States and United Kingdom under the Reagan and Thatcher governments in the 1980s, during which time domestic telecommunication and broadcasting markets were liberalized and privatized to a historic degree. In 1983, for example, Britain's formerly state-owned postal, telegraph and telephone utility was transferred to the private commercial firm British Telecom. In the 1990s, a wave of telecom privatization and deregulation swept through both North America and the European Union. The design for a similar project in regard to digital infrastructure and services was articulated in the G7's 1995 Global Information Infrastructure initiative, a plan that originated in the United States and has been described as 'an imperial triumph of unprecedented scope' (Raboy 2002: 127). The initiative 'enshrined a single vision, program and policy framework for the role of communication technology as a means of achieving an idealized global society driven by the market forces of transnational capital' (Raboy 2002: 127). This framework stressed the importance of private ownership of communications infrastructure, open markets for foreign trade, investment and competition, and regulatory relaxation as conditions of economic growth, job creation, innovation and competitiveness in the global economy. These values have been progressively enshrined in the expanding matrix of international trade and economic agreements, notably the WTO's Basic Agreement on Telecommunication Services and the General Agreement on Trade in Services, that together have constructed a global media and communication market on the neo-liberal model. Under this model, communication technologies, content and services are defined as commodities, thus leaving the transnational private actors that control them relatively free from the protectionist and interventionist regulatory designs of individual nation-states, including measures intended to secure public service obligations in the provision of communication services by private actors (D. Schiller 1999: 37–88).

The implications of the situation of the network society and its constitutive technologies, products and services in the neo-liberal political economy of globalization are significant. In the first place, it reflects the ongoing dominance of the global mediascape by commercial corporate media interests originating in the developed countries of the affluent North. As Jill Hills puts it, 'The enduring hallmark of the 1990s is the power wielded by multinationals in the drive for world economic integration, of which telecommunication is the vanguard' (Hills 1998: 119–20). Indeed, the pace of transnational combination and consolidation in the telecommunication and media sectors has been nothing short of extraordinary. It has been driven by the horizontal and vertical integration of firms across various media types (broadcasting, film and video, music recording, publishing, telephony) and across the divide that once separated firms engaged in content production from those that control the carriage infrastructure through which media products are accessed and distributed. The result is what has been described as a 'global media oligopoly' consisting of a decreasing handful of global titans and a somewhat broader array of national or regional conglomerates (Herman and McChesney 1997: 70).

This is linked to a second implication of the situation of the network society within the parameters of neo-liberal, capitalist globalization: the democratic liabilities of this political economy. As Murdock and Golding observe, the dynamics of neo-liberalism have 'massively increased the scale and scope of corporate reach in key communication sectors' (Murdock and Golding 2001: 114). This enhancement of the control enjoyed by private capital over communication infrastructure and services is matched by diminishing opportunities for institutionalized democratic expression and enforcement of the public interest in this sector, in those cases where that interest is not automatically reflected in the outcomes of the market. Thus, whatever potentials its instrumental uses might hold for democratic politics, network technology remains situated in a political economy in which a great deal of democratic, public control over communications – a crucial democratic resource – has devolved to the private calculations of massive corporate actors whose accountability is to shareholders and (more marginally) to consumers, rather than to citizens and their governments. In this respect, at least, the economy of the network society is one in which the already powerful find their power increased rather than significantly diminished.

A new economy?

As discussed in chapter 1, the idea that something like 'knowledge' or 'information' is central to late capitalism did not originate in the discourse surrounding the network society. Indeed, this idea also figured centrally in discourses proclaiming the arrival of 'Post-Industrial' and/or the 'Information' Society. It has, however, re-emerged with considerable force in contemporary characterizations of the network society. The central claim remains relatively unchanged from its genesis in theories of post-industrial society: the basis of economic life has shifted dramatically, not from capitalism to some other system, but rather from an economy driven by resource extraction and industrial manufacturing to one driven by the circulation and application of knowledge. Here, services (of an increasingly varied and ambiguously defined range) take up a central role in the economy, and information and knowledge assume apparently new prominence as productive resources and commodities. For most people, this purported shift to a new economy is most evident in relation to their experience of the world of employment. As May points out: 'The argument is clear: in this new information economy we work primarily with our minds rather than with our hands, and these jobs are best understood as service related, as the provision of information, the deployment of knowledge . . . In this new economy it is ideas that count, knowledge that is the important resource' (May 2002: 14). We shall return to the issue of the nature of work in the new economy below.

The relationship between new information and communication technologies and the new economy is central to the network society thesis, and cannot be overstated. As we will discuss below, network technologies are crucial to the coordination of the complex, territorially dispersed enterprises and decentralized firms that increasingly characterize the network economy. Beyond this however, it is also argued that these technologies have reoriented capitalist economies in a more fundamental, pervasive manner. According to Castells:

> The emergence of a new technological paradigm organized around new, more powerful and more flexible information technologies makes it possible for information itself to become the product of the production process. To be more precise: the products of new information technology industries are information processing devices or information processing itself. New information technologies, by transforming the processes of information processing, act upon all domains of human activity, and make it possible to establish endless connections between different domains, as well as between elements and agents of such activities. A networked, deeply interdependent economy emerges that becomes increasingly able to apply its progress in technology, knowledge and management to technology, knowledge and management themselves. (Castells 1996: 67)

It is in this sense that the new, knowledge-based economy is understood not as replacing or eliminating industrial, resource-based enterprises, economies and occupations but, rather, as encompassing these in economic networks in which the technologically mediated circulation and application of information is a defining attribute. Thus, industrial enterprises – such as, for example, auto manufacturing, mining or agribusiness – insofar as they are linked communicatively in complex intra- and inter-firm networks, employ technologically skilled labourers and deploy complex information technologies in their processes and operations, are part of, not distinct from, the new economy of the network society.

So-called 'new economies' are characterized by a considerable variety of indicators, most of which are somehow related to the expansive economic role played by new information and communication technologies. These include:

- escalating productivity of technology sectors and technology-intensive industries;
- growing markets for commodified information/knowledge products and services;
- transnational organization of firms, markets and services;
- increased technological mediation of commercial and financial activity (i.e., 'e-commerce');
- increasing demands for highly skilled labour/'knowledge-workers';
- elevated importance of skills education and training (i.e., 'lifelong learning');
- continued growth of service/information-processing employment;
- restructuring of work and employment in response to the imperatives/possibilities of information technology;
- innovation and research and development as drivers of economic growth and competitiveness;
- proliferation of new models of 'flexible' production and management;
- growing 'digital divides' between those who are positioned to take advantage of network technology and those who are not.

These conditions, to varying degrees, are believed to pertain wherever something called the 'new economy' appears. Each of them is inextricable from the proliferation and development of new information and communication technologies.

The last point on the list enumerated above merits elaboration here, as it indicates a crucial, systemic element of the new economy of the network society. It refers to that feature of new economies whereby material and political polarization intensifies between those who are effectively integrated into technological and economic networks and those who are excluded from them. This polarization pertains *intra*-nationally between individuals within economically advantaged countries, between regions within countries, and internationally between affluent and poor countries. In every case, connection correlates with affluence and influence, and disconnection with poverty and powerlessness. The structural characteristics of the network society include a logic of exclusion in which technological disconnection corresponds to political and economic disenfranchisement. Thus, Castells writes of 'black holes of informational capitalism' that comprise the Fourth World of the global network society. This Fourth World is a diverse constellation of geographic areas and individuals linked by their common exclusion from global networks of technology, wealth and power. It encompasses the impoverished nations of Africa, Latin America and Asia, but is also present in the various marginalized populations of 'every country, and every city' (Castells 1998: 164). As Castells observes, 'the rise of the Fourth World is inseparable from the rise of informational, global capitalism' (Castells 1998: 165) – it is, in this sense, a part of the new economy that has a great deal in common with the old economy.

As suggested in chapter 1, many people contest the notion of a new, knowledge-based economy. Some think it trades on a dubious conception of knowledge (knowledge as information, knowledge as skill/expertise, knowledge as technology/technique); others feel that the idea of a knowledge economy exaggerates the purported demise of capitalism's industrial base, which remains central to most capitalist economies, even those where new technologies are widely present. It is also sometimes argued that every economy is a knowledge economy, to the extent that no effective execution of productive human labour is possible without an organization of the knowledge entailed in that effort. Finally, critics charge that the rhetoric of the 'new economy' obscures the basic continuities of the old capitalist economy that are present even in technologically saturated environments. In this view, terms like 'post-industrial economy', 'new economy' and 'knowledge economy' are more ideological and promotional than descriptive. That is, though it purports to provide an objective, neutral account of a set of dynamics that is simply happening around us whether we like it or not, some suggest the discourse of the new economy actually serves to demand, justify and reify a particular reorganization of economic life that is, in fact, contingent rather than necessary (May 2002: 8).

Nevertheless, states throughout the world, and especially the governments of the affluent world, have adopted the discourse of the new-economy without reservation. At this level, promotion of what have been identified as key ingredients of the new-economy recipe has become a seemingly non-negotiable aspect of material success in the contemporary context. A typical example of national approaches to the new economy is contained in the British government's 1998 White Paper entitled *Our Competitive Future: Building the Knowledge Driven Economy*. Here, the imperative to nurture a new economy is expressed with considerable clarity:

> In the increasingly global economy of today, we cannot compete in the old way. Capital is mobile, technology can migrate quickly and goods can be made in low cost countries and shipped to developed markets. Britain must compete by exploiting capabilities which its competitors cannot easily match or imitate. These distinctive capabilities are not raw materials, land, or access to cheap labour. They must be knowledge, skills and creativity, which help create high productivity business processes and high value goods and services. That is why we will only compete successfully in future if we create an economy that is genuinely 'knowledge driven'. (United Kingdom 1998a: 10)

Thus, the British government commits itself to the development of a 'knowledge driven economy', which it defines as 'one in which the generation and the exploitation of knowledge has come to play the predominant part in the creation of wealth. It is not simply about pushing back the frontiers of knowledge; it is also about the more effective use and exploitation *of all types of knowledge in all manner of economic activity*' (United Kingdom 1998b: 2; emphasis original). Echoing governments in developed countries the world over, Britain sees a robust knowledge economy as crucial to competitiveness, job creation, and economic growth.

This commitment to develop a knowledge-driven economy brings with it a particular conception of the role and responsibility of the state in establishing conditions under which such an economy might flourish. Again, the British government's White Paper is exemplary in its articulation of this vision of the state's role. High on the list is a concerted effort to establish and maintain a hospitable climate for investment, entrepreneurialism and risk-taking. The key goal here is to support 'innovation' – not simply producing more of the same thing, but producing new and better things in new and better ways. The measures envisioned as necessary to generate a culture of innovation include relatively widespread deregulation and market liberalization (especially in sectors related to telecommunication and technology; typically styled as promoting 'competition'); tax relief and other incentives, such as relaxed thresholds for insolvency, to encourage investment of venture capital; increased public expenditure on research and technology development; active encouragement of the commercialization of scientific research; provision of an infrastructure for collaboration, partnership, clustering and best practices at the national, regional, local and sectoral levels; and configuration of intellectual property regimes to support product development. A second set of measures revolves around the state's management of the relationship between education and the economy. To serve a knowledge-driven economy, it is proposed, education must be more carefully articulated with the needs of enterprise and industry. This means, primarily, a shift in emphasis towards education as skills-training, both the 'hard' skills required of technicians in high-tech industry and the so-called 'soft' skills of communication, adaptability, decision-making, risk assessment and teamwork required for success in the agile, flexible enterprises of the new economy. It also involves the promotion of new models of education delivery, including technologically mediated 'lifelong' and 'distance' learning, which seek to facilitate the continual retraining and ongoing qualification required of workers in a technologically dynamic labour market. Finally, it is also perceived as imperative that the state actively develops its technological and legal infrastructure to support the proliferation of electronic commerce, in its various manifestations (online shopping, business-to-business transactions, enterprise networks, etc.).

This, as the Prime Minister, Tony Blair, describes in his foreword to the White Paper, comprises 'a new approach to industrial policy', one which charts 'the route to commercial success and prosperity for all' (United Kingdom 1998a: 5). The British approach is indeed representative of a consensus shared by most liberal-capitalist states as to the imperatives of success in the new economy. Not everyone, however, shares the Prime Minister's sanguine view of the destiny of the new economy. Many, in fact, understand the new economy as little more than an acceleration, extension and deepening of the basic operation, structure and relations of the old capitalist economy, accomplished under the ideological cover of perceived technological imperatives emanating from the development of global digital networks (Barney 2000; McChesney et al. 1998; Robins and Webster 1999; D. Schiller 1999). Indeed, it has been argued that the range of measures outlined above are all best understood as manifestations of a concerted drive to unburden global capitalism and capitalists from the obligations enforced upon them by the development of national welfare states. The new economy is, in this view, one in which the state has been fairly restored to the role of handmaiden to capital, a role from which it had somewhat departed in the half-century following the Great Depression of the 1930s. This is not to say that the state is, or has become, impotent in the new economy. Under the banner of 'competitiveness' states have, in fact, been very active in identifying the conditions of private accumulation with public welfare, building an infrastructure and labour force prepared for flexibility and innovation, bolstering national champions ready for clashes in global markets, and encouraging investment. The 'new' economy of the network society can be understood, at least partially, as the technological completion of this agenda.

Network enterprise

According to Castells, 'the most important transformation underlying the emergence of a global economy concerns the management of production and distribution, and of the production process itself' (Castells 1996: 96). In chapter 1, the transition from the Fordist to the post-Fordist regime of economic accumulation and regulation was described in terms of a shift from mass standardization to flexible customization as a core value of production, distribution and consumption. In this context, the model of the network – a web of semi-autonomous nodes interconnected by multiple, easily reconfigured ties through which a variety of flows can pass – and the technologies of networked computers emerge as a combination particularly apt for achieving flexibility in economic activity. Indeed, this combination gives rise to what Castells describes as a new organizational logic characteristic of economic activity in the network society: the network enterprise.

In contrast with the hierarchical, centralized, isolated, territorially defined corporation and the rigid, standardized chains of in-house production, supply and distribution characteristic of the Fordist mass production paradigm, in the network society 'the network is the enterprise' (Castells 2001: 67). Here is how Castells describes the network enterprise:

> [It is] the organizational form built around business projects resulting from the cooperation between different components of different firms, networking among themselves for the duration of a given business project, and reconfiguring their networks for the implementation of each project . . . Thus, the network enterprise is neither a network of enterprises nor an intra-firm networked organization. Rather it is a lean agency of economic activity, built around specific business projects, which are enacted by networks of various composition and origin . . . While the firm continues to be the unit of accumulation of capital, property rights and strategic management, business practice is performed by ad-hoc networks. These networks have the flexibility and adaptability required by a global economy subjected to relentless technological innovation and stimulated by rapidly changing demand. (Castells 2001: 67)

The network enterprise is thus a deterritorialized (though sometimes regionalized) network of networks of economic nodes, a formation whose architecture resembles that of the advanced digital communication technologies that make it possible. These constellations are comprised of overlapping intra- and inter-firm production and distribution networks (in which small and medium-sized firms cooperate with large ones), temporary strategic and sectoral alliances between large (even competing) firms with common interests, and relatively immediate (though spatially distanced) relationships between vendors and consumers. Combined with flexible, just-in-time production and delivery systems, novel marketing strategies aimed at maximizing consumers' perceptions of personalization and customization within the framework of a familiar brand, and horizontal management strategies aimed at melding limited autonomy for nodes (i.e., workers, managers, partners, 'teams') with enhanced centralized control, these arrangements make for a mode of organization agile enough to thrive under the conditions of post-Fordist, global capitalism.

As suggested above, the 'network enterprise' is a term that actually gathers a number of related organizational forms. Perhaps first among these is the *internal decentralized networking of large firms*. The network enterprise is said to be one in which the hierarchies of traditionally organized firms have been flattened into horizontal networks of interdependent, self-managing 'teams'. Centralized, bureaucratic, hierarchical authority structures, with their formal processes and many layers of middle management, are simply not agile or flexible enough to adapt quickly to changing demand cycles, markets and technological innovations. Horizontal, relatively decentralized networks are far easier to reconfigure than are established hierarchies. Production practices organized on the network model are leaner and more flexible than those organized hierarchically. Also, in a knowledge and innovation saturated economy, it is not always easy to predict when one part of an organization will need to be able to cooperate functionally with another part in a timely, effective manner in order to meet the goals of a particular project or strategy. Separating the various functions within an organization in airtight containers connected to one another only through vertically organized levels of bureaucracy is cumbersome and slow – not nearly agile enough for dynamic operations under dynamic conditions. Decentralized intra-firm networking of project-oriented teams committed to 'total quality' is the norm of the network enterprise.

A second crucial element of the network enterprise model is *multilocational, segmented production and distribution chains*, both within firms and in 'outsourced' partnerships. One of the outcomes of economic globalization is that national economies now find themselves engaged in 'locational tournaments' in which they compete for productive investment by creating an attractive environment for firms (i.e., low wage rates, tax relief, loans and subsidies, a trained and disciplined workforce, an unobtrusive regulatory climate, etc.) (Deibert 1997: 156). In this milieu, firms have incentives to move various parts of their operation to locations that provide the best conditions for profitability. Thus, many large enterprises now organize their chains of production as multilocational, transnational networks, with various elements of a finished product produced and assembled in a multiplicity of locations. In some cases, these territorially dispersed networks operate under the auspices of a single firm, in many cases they are simply a network of relatively independent producers, manufacturers or service providers contracted to provide a particular component or service that is ultimately labelled with a single brand. What is significant about these arrangements is their adaptability: networked chains of production can be reconfigured to respond to innovation, or changing demand, with far greater ease than a large operation fixed under one roof in a single location. Nodes can also be abandoned and/or relocated when conditions elsewhere become more attractive, without compromising the integrity of the entire enterprise.

A third manifestation of the network enterprise model is the proliferation of *networks of small and medium-sized firms linked to larger networks*. This is the so-called 'Benetton Model', named for the Italian knitwear company that rose to global prominence based on a network of small (sometimes even home-based) producers linked with the brand's global chain of retail outlets. The network model does not apply only to large, transnational firms, but also to small and medium-sized firms that specialize in certain niche areas and make their profits by connecting to larger networks that contract for their products and services, either as individual small nodes or as part of small constellations of nodes with other small firms. Together, these smaller operations are able to engage in the kinds of specialized, flexible production practices that are necessary in an economy marked by customization and constant innovation. Their existence also relieves large firms of the burden of maintaining large inventories in order to realize economies of scale – a risky proposition in the context of markets whose profitability is premised on customization, short demand cycles and constant novelty. Networking at the business-to-business level includes highly efficient supplier–client relationships wherein suppliers provide customized elements of the production process rapidly (just-in-time) and thus free the client from the risk of maintaining excessive inventory. This, of course, requires productive practices within these networks of small firms that are themselves highly flexible.

A fourth characteristic of the network enterprise model is the growing importance of *sectoral-level strategic alliances and project-driven, ad hoc joint ventures between firms.*

Along with its basis in the intra-firm networking of large firms and organizations, and the business-to-business networking of small and medium-sized firms connected to larger firms and networks, the network enterprise is also marked by the proliferation of inter-firm networking between erstwhile competitors at the sectoral level, often in ad hoc joint ventures and temporary strategic alliances around specific projects. This tendency casts the network economy as a strange amalgamation of cooperation and competition – strange only if we are operating under the assumptions of Fordism with its relatively isolated firms competing in markets with stable and fixed parameters. Under *post*-Fordist conditions, such isolation is too risky to be sustained, and not profitable enough to be risked. Castells description of this dynamic is evocative:

> The structure of high technology industries in the world is an increasingly complex web of alliances, agreements, and joint ventures in which most large corporations are interlinked . . . Their actual operations are conducted with other firms: not only with the hundreds or thousands of subcontracting and ancillary enterprises, but with the dozens of relatively equal partners with whom they cooperate and compete at the same time in this brave new economic world where friends and foes are the same. (Castells 1996: 163)

In 2000, for example, fourteen of the world's largest mining and metals companies announced the creation of an internet-based venture to facilitate the more efficient and cost-effective buying and selling of mining supplies. Though these firms are rivals in the mining and metals business, they have recognized their common interests in reducing the costs of doing business, through a joint venture such as this. In this light, it is not difficult to see why organizational decentralization of production in the network economy is understood by many to represent a significant concentration of power and interest at the highest registers of global capitalism, even in the midst of the rhetoric of 'competition' that characterizes this economy's liberal imagination of itself.

The final aspect of the network enterprise model is the growth of *networks of synchronous interactivity between consumers/customers and vendors/firms* – networks that are indispensable to the cycles of mass customization and personalization characteristic of the consumption side of the network economy. Here, individual consumers act as nodes in the productive enterprise by feeding information back into it – crucial marketing and preference information that spurs innovation and enables enterprises to navigate demand and deliver 'customized' products and services at 'customized' prices. What is interesting here is that the flow between the customer nodes and the enterprise nodes is reciprocal: it is not just that customers receive flows (i.e. products); they also contribute flows (information) that become crucial in the success of the entire enterprise, and are necessary for the mass personalization and short product cycles upon which the entire model sits. Much of this occurs automatically via the consumer surveillance utilities built into most electronic commerce interfaces. Thus, whether they are actively configuring a product to their preferences, or signalling these unintentionally via automated data transmissions, customers engaged in e-commerce in its various forms now perform a considerable amount of unpaid market research and design work for the firms that sell them products. This, in many respects, is emblematic of the particular genius of the network enterprise model.

Various aspects of the network enterprise model can be found in operation across economic sectors. Prominent examples include computer and communication firms such as Dell, Nokia and Cisco, companies who manage a brand but hold little inventory, whose products combine components from a network of literally hundreds of separate suppliers across the globe, and who deliver relatively customized packages to consumers, often through online interfaces accessible via the world wide web. Retail operations of various kinds (food, clothing, books and music) not only conduct commerce via the internet, they are also embedded in complex and dynamic networks with suppliers and distributors, as well as networks of small-scale operators who produce the wide range of items that end up with an in-house brand. Even traditional manufacturing enterprises – e.g., aviation, automobile, clothing and weapons industries – have reconfigured on this model, adopting intra- and inter-firm networks, establishing complex global supply, production and distribution networks, engaging in strategic joint ventures within their own sector but across national boundaries, taking advantage of the commercial possibilities of electronically mediated sales, advertising and merchandising. And a wide range of services, including banking, energy, finance, travel, healthcare and education have followed suit. Thus, despite the recent ill fortunes of the inflated 'dot-com economy' and 'tech boom', the network enterprise seems to be settling in as the organizational model of post-Fordist capitalism.

Of course, crucial to the success of this model has been the proliferation of digital information and communication technologies. Without these, the organization and operation of the network enterprise model sketched above would simply be impossible. Nick Dyer-Witheford paints a vivid picture of the triangular relationship between the network enterprise, network technology and the directing hand of capital:

> Electronic information systems in particular allow transnational corporations to decentralize operations while centralizing control; executives in Toronto offices open on-screen windows displaying the performance of machine operators in Seoul factories. Manufacturing strategies for products such as Ford's 'world car' rely on telecommunications to coordinate production flows at plants on different continents, as well as to perfect the standardization of modular parts . . . Global homework industries, such as those of Benetton, network computers to tie suppliers to sellers, match production to inventories, monitor dispersed workers, and check the quality and speed of supply through every rung of their hierarchy. The same logic, to a greater or lesser degree, allows Canadian supermarkets to sell fresh-cut flowers from Africa, or travel agencies in Bonn and Tokyo to book sex tours in Thailand and the Philippines. (Dyer-Witheford 1999: 136)

Network enterprises require a sophisticated control technology to ensure their effective and efficient operation. Contrary to the idea that Taylorist, scientific management has been replaced by decentralized self-management, network technologies have enabled a decentralization of operations in the midst of an expansion and intensification of the power of centralized management and control (Robins and Webster 1999: 11–130; Rochlin 1997: 51–73). As May puts it, 'Certainly, information, surveillance and efficiency, the very principles of Taylorism have become intensified, extended and automated through the application of new communication and information technologies. Scientific management has been enhanced by the information revolution, not rendered obsolete' (May 2002: 69).

This is not to suggest that the advent of new information and communication technologies *caused* the reorganization of economic activity on the network model. At most, this relationship is a reciprocal one, with the new organizational form demanding enhanced communicative capacities, and the technological innovations rising to meet these demands in turn spurring further refinement and entrenchment of network logic on an organizational level. What is clear is that the network business model is information and communication intensive, requiring rapid (ideally automated) and reliable exchange, storage, retrieval and processing of massive volumes of process-relevant data, unfettered by geographic distance – precisely what is enabled by digital computer networks and their related technologies. These new information and communication technologies form the indispensable infrastructure of the network enterprise, whereby economic activity can be dispersed in decentralized, dynamic networks of operation that nevertheless remain firmly under centralized surveillance and control.

Network work

In capitalist society, most people must work for a living, and many of the most significant economic effects of network technology have been, and continue to be, felt in the structure and practice of everyday work and employment. This speaks to the comprehensive nature of digital technologies, which are not only instruments of communication and information but also, crucially, instruments of production. And, just as these technologies have been central to a restructuring of the organization of capitalist enterprise at the level of the firm, so too have they mediated significant changes in the structure of employment and in the organization and practice of work in capitalist economies. In this respect, the network technologies of digitized bar-code scanners at supermarket checkouts and networked computer reservation systems in call centres are perhaps more significant, in material terms, than the technologies of online chat services, interactive entertainment websites, and electronic voting.

Networks and (un)employment

The contours of the relationship between network technology, employment and work are complex and varied. In the early stages of the development of network technology and its application to productive processes, a great deal of debate was generated around the prospect of a rise in levels of technologically induced unemployment. Networked computers are technologies of automation par excellence, and where automation leads, so the argument goes, a displacement of human labour follows. These fears were mirrored by an official discourse – at both nation-state and global levels – surrounding the development of new information and communication technologies that connected them unambiguously with economic growth and job creation.

Resolving the question of whether digital technologies are job killers or job creators has proved difficult. On the one hand, it is certain that the automation and reconfiguration of tasks enabled by computer technology has certainly displaced large numbers of working people from their jobs, because tasks that once required a direct application of human labour can now be accomplished entirely by a computerized device, by fewer employees because of the productive efficiencies afforded by computerization, or by management remotely using a computer (Menzies 1996: 59–69). Thus do the jobs of telephone operators and receptionists disappear, the number of positions on automobile assembly lines get reduced, and the jobs of floor-level supervisors get assumed by remote middle managers using automated workplace surveillance technologies. Critics also warn that it is misleading to separate new information technologies from other dynamics that render employment precarious in the contemporary economic climate. Even in cases where it is not possible to link job loss or unemployment directly to a specific technology, it is the case that digital technology is deeply implicated in, for example, the mobility of production operations and capital, a type of 'flow' that often washes away employment in its wake. When a manufacturing operation moves 'offshore' to capitalize on lower wage rates or deregulation or low taxes, it results in job loss at the original site of production. If it is digital technology that enables the transnationalization and fragmenting of the enterprise in this way, by enabling physical relocation without severing the operation from the firm's network, then is digital technology contributing to net employment or net unemployment? Critics say that to understand how digital technology is affecting employment levels we have to look at the role the technology plays in the economic dynamics of globalization more generally – many of which are causes of deep instability in the labour market.

On the other hand, it is undeniable that countries where network technology is most highly developed and widespread have not suffered catastrophic, or even rising, levels of unemployment as a result of technological advance. In its *World Employment Report 2001*, the International Labour Organization (ILO) points to a 'major turnaround in employment fortunes' in OECD countries, where 'overall unemployment has declined sharply' in the 1990s, over the very same period that network technology penetrated the economies of those countries (International Labour Organization 2001: 1). Nevertheless, the report also points out that 'despite the communications revolution taking place in the world today, increasing numbers of workers are unable to find jobs', referring to the fact that in 2001 roughly one-third of the world's workforce of 3 billion people remained unemployed (International Labour Organization 2001: 1). In this sense, the global economy structured at least partly by network technology has hardly been a boon for employment. Still, the ILO – echoing the now-standard chorus of numerous similar organizations – is unambiguous in its endorsement of a more generalized development of advanced communication technologies as a *remedy* for systemic unemployment in the developing economies, provided the deployment of these technologies is supported by strategies aimed at enabling marginalized populations to use them to their own advantage, rather than disadvantage.

Thus, the consensus seems to be that, in the aggregate, network technologies do not have the deleterious effect on rates of employment that early critics feared they would. Echoing the discourses of post-industrialism and the information society, Castells argues that it is the *characteristics*, rather than the *level*, of employment in societies where network technology has proliferated that are significant. Referring to the G7 countries, he identifies several trends in this regard: the phasing out of agricultural employment and a steady decline in manufacturing jobs; the rise and diversification of the service sector (broadly defined to include business, social, commercial, entertainment, leisure and personal services) as the dominant source of employment; and the simultaneous expansion of upper (managerial, professional, technical) and lower (clerical, retail and personal services) levels in the occupational structure (Castells 1996: 228–9). In regard to this last point, Castells adds that the rate of expansion in the upper registers of the occupational structure is outpacing growth at the lower registers, resulting in a 'relative upgrading of the occupational structure over time' (Castells 1996: 229).

Needless to say, these characterizations of the status of employment in the advanced 'information' economies of the network society have not gone uncontested. Christopher May, for example, argues persuasively that accounts of a qualitative and quantitative shift to a new, post-industrial service economy replete with information-professionals rely heavily on a set of conceptual allowances that are somewhat questionable. These include definitions of service work that insufficiently differentiate between the wide variety of occupations that purportedly are gathered under this category;

assumptions that jobs are 'information' intensive only when they involve computers (and that all jobs that do so are information occupations); and statistical models that too easily accept change in the nominal title of a job as evidence of a change in the status of that occupation (May 2002: 53–66). It is not clear, after all, that 'service employment' is a very meaningful category if it includes both the bank manager and the person who sells her coffee during her cigarette breaks, or that the job of an airline reservation agent is more 'information intensive' than that of a school custodian simply because her daily tasks are conducted using complex digital devices, or that a clerk registering customer complaints by telephone somehow becomes 'managerial' when his job is retitled 'consumer relationship manager'. At the very least, attempts to characterize changes in the structure of employment at the macro-level in network societies must be supplemented by careful attention to the micro-level particularities that either distort or confirm those broader projections.

Networks and the restructuring of work and employment

Less contested than the impact of network technology on employment is the widespread consensus that these technologies have been intimately involved in a restructuring of the practice and organization of work in advanced capitalist economies. As Barbara Crow and Graham Longford point out, 'Digitalization has affected the *nature of work* performed in the economy as much as the *quantity of employment*' (Crow and Longford 2000: 211; emphasis added). Indeed, there is little doubt that network technology has been instrumental to a fairly significant restructuring of work, and its relationship to employment, in line with the needs of the global post-Fordist economy and the network enterprises that drive it. As discussed above, the central operating principle and core organizational value of the post-Fordist economy is *flexibility*. We have discussed how flexibility has been achieved in the organization of firms, production and finance – largely through their reconstitution in the form of networks mediated by digital technology. What remains to be discussed is the achievement of flexibility in human *labour* – largely through the reconstitution of work and workplaces according to the network model and the mediation of work by digital network technologies.

The organization of labour and work on the welfare-state/industrial model was oriented towards security rather than flexibility. It featured well-defined, relatively permanent job classifications and long-term obligations to employees – both skilled and unskilled – often entrenched in labour codes or binding collective agreements that were difficult to amend or infringe. The standard form of employment was a full-time, permanent job completed at regular hours on a relatively fixed schedule, at a place of employment maintained by the employer. People were trained or educated in a set of skills at the outset of their working life, and typically pursued careers along a fairly constrained path, often remaining in the same job for the same firm for the bulk of their working life, or pursuing mobility upwards in the hierarchy of the firm. In most jurisdictions, state-administered unemployment insurance served (among other things) to mitigate the disciplinary threat of imminent unemployment. Work, in this sense, was *institutionalized*. It just sounds inflexible.

Human labour remains an indispensable part of contemporary economies, but the demands of flexibility – enforced by an economy whose growth depends on perpetual innovation and customization – have transformed labour and work in radical ways. Like all other parts of the network enterprise, labour has had to be configured as adaptable, diversified, agile, easily redeployed, and operationally decentralized while remaining under centralized control. Work in the network economy has been radically deinstitutionalized and 'individualized' in order that it might become more flexible, and so more responsive to the demands of adaptability that motivate the network enterprise as a whole. Based on a survey of labour market trends across the advanced capitalist economies, which provides clear evidence of generalized (with the notable exception of Japan) ascendance of non-standard, flexible, contingent forms of employment, Castells concludes that 'the traditional form of work, based on full-time employment, clear cut occupational assignments, and a career pattern over the lifecycle, is being slowly but surely eroded away' (Castells 1996: 268). This 'flexibilization' of labour has a number of manifestations, each of which merits some closer scrutiny here.

These various phenomena are best described under the rubric of *non-standard forms of employment*. Above, the standard form of employment under the Fordist industrial regime was defined as a full-time, permanent job, completed at regular hours on a relatively fixed schedule, at a place of employment maintained by the employer, typically on a fairly linear career path. As Castells suggests, this standard is no longer descriptive of the arrangements under which increasing numbers of people work. Instead, more flexible, 'non-standard' or 'contingent' (i.e., uncertain) employment arrangements have become the new standard. Chief among these arrangements are *part-time work and temporary work*, the latter representing, for example, the fastest growing sector of the American labour force. Tellingly, by 1998, Manpower – a temporary employment agency – was the largest single employer in the United States, with 600,000 people on payroll (compared with 400,000 at General Motors and 350,000 at IBM), and temporary employment agencies are also among Europe's fastest growing companies. Statistics such as these have led critics such as Naomi Klein to describe the 'rented worker' as one of the fastest growing categories of employment in North America and Europe (Klein 2000: 247).

The second form of non-standard employment on the rise in the network society is *self-employment and episodic contract work, consulting or 'freelancing'*, in which workers move from one short-term performance contract to the next without a long-term arrangement with a single employer (Vosko 2000). As discussed above in relation to the category of service work, the designation 'self-employed' actually represents a wide array of diverse work situations, ranging from professionals, to small-business owners, to independent craftworkers and tradespeople, to contract or piece-based service workers. And across these categories there is further significant division between those who also employ others and those who work solely as individuals. Nevertheless, it is clear that self-employment has grown dramatically since the

1980s, its rate of growth outpacing that of paid employment in fifteen out of twenty-four OECD countries over the period ranging from 1979 to 1997 (Fudge et al. 2002). Indeed, all of the forms of non-standard work arrangements mentioned above are increasing significantly in all advanced economies (Carnoy 2000). It is also worth pointing out that these forms of non-standard employment are increasingly prevalent in the high-tech and service sectors so central to the economy of the network society, and that women – and this pertains to almost all forms of non-standard work arrangements – are dramatically over-represented in the contingent labour force both globally and in most national jurisdictions (Benner and Dean 2000: 361; Vosko 2000). As Castells puts it: 'As a general trend, the "organization man" is out, the "flexible woman" is in' (Castells 2001: 95).

A third set of characteristics typical of the restructuring of work into non-standard forms coheres around what could be described as *the temporal and spatial dislocation of work*. *Temporal dislocation* refers to employment arrangements in which paid work is not confined within the parameters of the eight-hour, nine-to-five day, and forty-hour, Monday-to-Friday work week. Instead, working time under the non-standard arrangements characteristic of the network economy is increasingly 'flex-time', wherein work is not organized according to a fixed, standardized schedule, but rather continuously adapted to the ebb and flow of demands. Here, work time is made flexible – twelve hours today and three tomorrow; a seventy-hour schedule this week and twenty the next; three two-hour shifts interspersed with childcare and domestic duties rather than a single six-hour shift; graveyard rather than daytime shifts, to accommodate the needs of customers four time-zones away – to meet the time-compressed character of contemporary global and domestic markets. According to Castells, 'between one-quarter and one-third of the employed population of the major industrialized countries does not follow the classic pattern of a full-time job with a regular working schedule . . . the prevailing trend in most advanced sectors of most advanced economies is the general diversification of working time' (Castells 1996: 442).

Spatial dislocation refers to the carrying out of work in physical locations other than more or less permanent, central

facilities or worksites provided and maintained by employers. Spatially dislocated work encompasses a wide range
of work practices, including homework, call-centre work
(in which labourers are centralized but work is spatially
dislocated into electronic networks), 'telework' (computer-
mediated work conducted solely from a remote location
with no presence at a central worksite) or 'telecommuting'
(work conducted from home via computer periodically,
but generally located at a real, permanent worksite) (Gurstein
2001; Johnson 2003). It is important to recognize that
no single form of totally dislocated work has become the
new norm for working arrangements in technologically
advanced economies (Gillespie and Richardson 2000).
Nevertheless, multiple forms of spatially and temporally
dislocated work now routinely combine with more traditional, located work practices to form highly dynamic,
multiplex modes of work organization, in which networked information and communication technologies figure
quite highly, and in which work is not necessarily experienced
as something carried out during regular times at a regular
place.

Another manifestation of the de-standardization of work
in the new economy is the purported *eclipse of the lifetime
career in a single occupational trajectory or firm*. The idea of
a stable job – a long-term position requiring a stable, sus-
tainable, predictable skill, often within a single firm – and a
career – a well-defined, lifelong path for the development and
elaboration of one's livelihood along a consistent trajectory
– is reportedly a thing of the past in the network society. The
average American with two years of college training can now
expect to change jobs at least eleven times and have to fairly
radically revamp their skill set (i.e. not just fine-tune) at least
three times in the course of a forty-year working life. It is not
that there is no work, it is that work decreasingly unfolds
within the categories of job and career – categories that are
rapidly becoming relics in all but a few professions. Instead
of people with jobs tied to defined and stable career paths,
the inhabitants of the new economy are characterized as
'portfolio workers' (Handy 1994) – people who move from
one task, contract or project to the next, constructing a
network of portable experience, contacts and skills without

ever holding what would once have been characterized as a steady job.

A corollary to this move from careers to networks of projects, contracts, experience and capacities is an *increasing social emphasis on the value of so-called 'lifelong learning'*, or the constant upgrading of qualifications and 'skills', so as to maximize flexibility and mobility, and to ensure compatibility with the ever-changing technological and organizational demands of the network enterprise. For individuals, flexibility in the labour market means a willingness to adapt quickly and repeatedly to changing technological, skill and expertise requirements, rather than commit to a single, defined set of work capacities and skills developed at the outset of one's working life. The capacity for perpetual requalification corresponds to what Castells describes as a distinction between 'self-programmable' and 'generic' labour. Self-programmable labour is 'able to reprogram itself, in skills, knowledge, and thinking according to changing tasks in an evolving business environment. Self-programmable labour requires a certain type of education, in which the stock of knowledge and information accumulated in the worker's mind can be expanded and modified throughout his or her life' (Castells 2001: 90–1). Generic labour, on the other hand, 'is embodied in workers who do not have special skills, or special ability to acquire skills in the production process, other than those necessary to execute instructions from management. Generic labour can be replaced by machines, or by generic labour anywhere else in the world . . .' (Castells 2001: 94). The discourse of the network society emphasizes self-programmable labour and its continual reproduction via constant retraining (euphemized as 'lifelong learning') as central to its economic future. That being said, it remains clear that capital's ready access to vast pools of generic labour is every bit as crucial to the accumulation strategies of the network society as is access to various forms of highly skilled labour.

In some cases, digital technology often directly mediates the sort of non-standard work arrangements described above by enabling, for example, various spatially and temporally dislocated work practices and the delivery of 'lifelong learning'/retraining online. That being said, it would be wrong to suggest that digital technology has somehow caused the proliferation of contingent employment relationships, self-employment and the replacement of careers by portfolios. Instead, these have arisen as part of capital's strategic commitment to flexibility as an organizational solution to the limits of the Fordist, mass production economy, and network technologies have been instrumental to the realization of this commitment. In what ways are these arrangements flexible? They are organized, like much of the network enterprise, around short-term engagements; they undermine fixed job classifications and employment situations and the inflexible institutional arrangements that secure them (e.g., collective agreements, unemployment insurance regimes, etc.); they divest firms of considerable administrative costs and risk by distributing these amongst a network of individuated, dispersed workers/nodes towards which the firm has limited long-term obligations; they enable the rapid reconfiguration of a firm's workforce, practices and resources to suit innovation or customized demand; they direct individual qualification towards ongoing cultivation of 'soft', process-oriented job skills that are more portable than traditional, content-heavy trade skills (especially at lower registers of the network economy). This unburdening of the firm's responsibilities in the employment relationship – responsibilities for training; for providing a safe and healthy workplace; for contributing to health insurance, pension, unemployment insurance, vacation and other benefits; for abiding by rules concerning the duration of the working day and week – might be the primary motivation for the widespread shift to the deinstitutionalization of work in the network society.

Of course, this is not the picture that is painted by those who endorse the shift to non-standard employment as a sort of technologically enhanced liberation for the working classes. There is a significant discourse which suggests the flexibility realized by employers in structuring work in non-standard ways is also enjoyed by workers themselves – self-employed, creative, entrepreneurial knowledge-workers who are free to craft their own work situations, and to chart their own course in the labour market according to their needs, interests and capabilities, to be their own boss, work with their brains rather than their bodies, and increase their mobility, autonomy and job satisfaction. There is certainly cultural support for this view. Increasingly, staying put in the same job or with the same firm for an extended period of time is considered to be a mark of failure rather than success, signalling a lack of initiative, creativity, ambition and drive. In the current climate, no job is a destination and every project is a step on the way to some ever-evolving but undefined end. It is also interesting to consider the cultural value that has been built around flexibility in working arrangements. In the current climate, many young people see a secure, Monday-to-Friday, nine-to-five job as a life sentence instead of a life. One way to characterize this is to suggest that, in the post-materialist era of a generation that has never suffered war or depression, people will trade flexibility for security without much hesitation. Perhaps more likely, though, is that the discourse of the network society has succeeding in *defining flexibility as a condition of security*, and anything that compromises flexibility (such as, for example, trade unions) as security's enemy.

It is undeniable that many people experience non-standard work arrangements as empowering and liberating. Those who do so include people who are already advantageously placed in the labour market (genuine professionals; highly skilled workers), those who have the means to provide healthy working conditions for themselves in the absence of an employer, those for whom self-financed training and skill development is more of an investment than a material sacrifice, and those who find in non-standard work arrangements a flexibility that encourages/allows them to re-enter paid employment where otherwise they might not have. This latter category particularly pertains to women, many of whom succeed in making the transition from, or managing the balance between, unpaid domestic labour and paid employment because of the flexibility afforded by non-standard work arrangements such as part-time, home-based, or electronically mediated work. Indeed, Castells identifies the integration of women into the paid workforce as intimately related to the rise of non-standard work arrangements generally when he writes that 'flex-time and part-time have penetrated the contractual structures of working-time on the basis of women's work, largely to accommodate women's needs to combine their child-rearing endeavours and their working lives' (Castells 1996: 443). Later, observing that educated women are 'providing a major supply of skilled, flexible and autonomous labour, as required by the e-conomy', Castells concludes that 'the structural incorporation of women into the labour market has been the indispensable basis for the development of the new economy . . .' (Castells 2001: 93). One would be hard pressed to deny the progressive aspects of a labour market whose organizational attributes enabled the entry of increasing numbers of educated women into paid employment in significant occupations.

On the other hand, there is considerable reason to believe that the impact of non-standard, flexible work arrangements on the everyday working lives of ordinary people will not be unambiguously positive. At a minimum, the individualization of work has two faces: one face for those who either choose it freely or are positioned to capitalize on its potential for autonomy and satisfaction; and a second face that presents itself to those have no choice but to settle for non-standard work involuntarily, and to those who lack the means to make this situation a healthy one. Looking at this second face – arguably the one confronting the considerable majority of working people in the new economy – one sees de-standardization from a somewhat different perspective. From this view, flexibility appears as an uncoupling of work from stable employment and a steady income. It means structural insecurity, a cost borne disproportionately by individual workers, in an environment in which the welfare state's contribution to individual security has also been scaled back. It means individual rather than collective responsibility for routine, periodic un- or under-employment. It means competition, rather than solidarity, between individual workers, both domestically and internationally. It means social and economic isolation for people whose work routines are dislocated in space and time relative to others doing the same work or working for the same firm. It means shifting the costs of technology, work facilities and risk from employers to employees. It means work practices and working conditions insulated from public scrutiny and regulation. It means disqualification from the non-wage benefits that typically accompany full-time permanent employment. It means individuals bearing responsibility for the constant upgrading and retraining necessary to remain employable in a market in which rapid, successive technological innovation is the norm. In short, the other face of de-standardized work is one that excites considerable anxiety and vulnerability for those who look it in the eye on a daily basis.

It is this other face that has led many analysts to describe the labour market of the network society as structured by a prevailing dynamic of *polarization*. In general, this polarization is presented as evincing a gulf between well-educated, highly skilled, highly mobile, highly compensated and secure 'knowledge professionals' on the one hand, and an underclass of less skilled, trained-but-undereducated, peripheral, replaceable, poorly compensated and insecure 'information' and non-information workers on the other. This polarization can be detected both within the labour markets of the most developed network economies and between populations in an international division of labour in which marginalization, dependency, exploitation and market irrelevance continue to play structural roles. Of course, these divisions manifest in real, material consequences. The benefits of proliferating non-standard forms of work and employment are differentially distributed between those for whom flexibility is a source and reflection of continued advantage and power, and those who experience flexibility as a source and reflection of their continued disempowerment and disadvantage. It is this material reality that has led to criticisms of the restructuring of work in network societies as deeply gendered, with women disproportionately represented among those whose experience of de-standardization and flexibility is characterized by insecurity and exploitation, both within the developed economies and in the periphery (Crow and Longford 2000; Menzies 1996; Vosko 2000). The restructuring of work and employment that marks the network society seems to guarantee that the material goods of marketability, mobility, compensation, job security and satisfaction, healthy working conditions and autonomy will remain unequally distributed, and mirror existing inequalities, for a while yet.

Network property

No account of the contours of network capitalism would be complete without at least brief consideration of the status of property in the context of proliferating information and communication technologies, a matter that has emerged as central to the trajectory of the so-called new economy. Private property and the exchange relations that arise from its commodification have always been crucial to the operation and shape of capitalist economies and societies. It is also true that various forms of information and communication 'products' have long assumed the status of commodities open for exchange in free markets. Network technologies are said to have affected the status of information, knowledge and communication as property and commodities in two, somewhat contradictory, ways. In the first place, these technologies, and the markets in which they are situated, have provided the means and incentive for a historically unprecedented expansion of the commodification of information and knowledge. The sense that knowledge, information and communication in their various forms are increasingly 'for sale' as 'intellectual property' is definitive of the new economy. In the second place, the technical attributes of network technology are such that control over these commodities – which is crucial to their status as property exchangeable for money or other property – has purportedly been destabilized. Network technologies enable cheap, efficient duplication and rapid dissemination of information rendered in non-degraded digital form, by and to parties who are dispersed across territorial and legal jurisdictions, and who are not always easily identified or located. All this can make it difficult to limit access to commodified information, and to police those who transgress these limitations in unauthorized ways. Since the market value of commodities is a function of limiting access to those who pay for them, this presents a considerable problem for a knowledge-based economy that so heavily relies on the profitable circulation of information commodities. Perhaps the most high-profile instance of this problem has been recent controversies over peer-to-peer, online file swapping services such as Napster, which enable the circulation of information commodities (in this case, primarily recorded music) without compensation for the holders of rights to those commodities.

It is tempting to conclude that network technology fundamentally threatens the security of intellectual property and information commodities and that, consequently, it undermines the capitalist foundations of the network economy. Indeed, Stewart Brand's provocative declaration that 'Information wants to be free' (Brand 1987: 202) remains the clarion call of a loose coalition of interests that sees in network technologies the potential for a non-proprietary alternative to the commercial development of digital media. Included here are the partisans of peer-to-peer file swapping, 'freeware' and 'shareware', open-source software coding, general public licensing, 'freenets', and a range of other non-proprietary technological applications and protocols. Castells specifies this 'hacker ethic' as foundational to 'the culture of the Internet': 'Paramount in this set of values is freedom. Freedom to create, freedom to appropriate whatever knowledge is available, and freedom to redistribute this knowledge under any form and channel chosen by the hacker' (Castells 2001: 46–7). The proliferation of this ethic instantiates a 'gift culture' that culminates in a 'gift economy' that directly challenges and contradicts the commodification of information in the network environment.

Nevertheless, requiems for the collapse of commerce, commodification and private property in the information age are premature at best. For, while it is true that network technology can pose challenges for the enforcement of intellectual property rights, and that network media hold out the prospect of an economy in which information is non-proprietary and its circulation non-commercial, it is also true that capital has responded vigorously to these very challenges and prospects (Lessig 2001; Vaidhyanthan 2001). Major established holders of intellectual property rights – e.g., content providers in the mass entertainment and publishing industries; software companies – have engaged a multifaceted strategy to combat what they portray as a fundamental threat to their property rights, to innovation and to free enterprise in general. This strategy has included pressing for legislative extension of intellectual property rights (especially copyright) and a roll-back of fair-use exceptions; designing and marketing technology and storage media which disable un-licensed duplication and distribution of copyrighted material; intimidating those who 'violate' copyright (especially activists) by bringing punitive litigation against them, in the hopes of accomplishing more generalized deterrence; and, perhaps most effectively, consolidating corporate control over the generation and circulation of valued forms of intel-lectual property through horizontal and vertical integration across the content/carriage divide. Taken together, these tactics drive a dynamic of concentration in control over intel-lectual property in the network society, and put paid to rumours of the imminent death of the information commod-ity. What we have witnessed in the information age is a 'remaking of information as property *despite its potential free availability*' (May 2002: 72; emphasis added). Ironically, those who have benefited most from this retrenchment of property rights have made great rhetorical use of the spectre of rampant, technologically mediated piracy in their efforts to persuade governments of the need to act decisively in their favour, in order to ensure the viability of the knowledge economy.

This chapter began with the observation that, whatever else it may be, the network society is a capitalist society. If it helps to think of this social formation as the outcome of some sort of revolution (and I am not sure it does help to think of it this way), we must at least bear in mind that it must have been a sort of revolution that left the basic foundations of capitalist economics – a division of labour that results in inequalities of power, advantage and wealth; social relations built on private property and commodity exchange; a com-mercial culture – decidedly intact. Indeed, the foregoing review of the dynamics of globalization, the 'knowledge' economy, the restructuring of work, and the consolidation of control over intellectual property suggests that, if anything, network capitalism is a supercharged version of its former self. That being said, this review should also make clear that the network economy is not therefore *exactly the same* as the capitalisms that have preceded it historically. An appre-ciation of our present situation requires that we reckon with both the continuities that link this species of capitalism with its predecessors, and the discontinuities that distinguish it from them. This can only be accomplished when our view is cleared of the ideological fog typically produced by rhetoric of revolution, especially when that rhetoric is wielded by those whose interests lie primarily in revolution's opposite.

4
Network Politics

Without the printing press there would have been no Reformation and no Enlightenment, or so the story goes. And no
nation-state, either, by the way. Communication technologies
have long been understood as central to the practices and
organization of politics, and network technologies are no
exception. Communication, after all, is essential to political
life. Politics combines judgement and action on public
matters, and neither judgement nor action can be wholly
divorced from communication, though it is true that certain
regimes engage in more communicative forms of public
judgement and action than others do. Liberal democracies,
for example, despite their imperfections relative to the
strongest standards of democracy, have historically relied on
communication in their practices of public judgement and
public action to a greater extent than tyrannies. In a liberal
democracy, communication in forms ranging from simple
registration of preferences to more robust deliberation is,
formally at least, considered indispensable to the practice of
public judgement and to the authorization of public action.
Those actions, furthermore, often take communicative forms,
such as the publication of laws, the delivery of education, the
dispensation of services, and the various arts of persuasion,
propaganda and protest that together occupy so much
political space in contemporary liberal democracies.
Consequently, the technologies that mediate communication

contribute substantially to the possibilities of politics in any given context. The technicalities of the printing press – a decentralized instrument capable of mass producing relatively cheap, portable documents – was a crucial enabler of the politics that drove the Reformation and Enlightenment in Europe (Edwards 1994; Eisenstein 1983; Febvre and Martin 1976; Gellner 1992). It also contributed to the consolidation of political identity and sovereign authority at the level of the nation-state, via the standardization of national vernaculars and the materialization, *in documents*, of the depersonalized authority of the state (Anderson 1983; Deibert 1997: 86–92; Febvre and Martin 1976: 319–32; Gellner 1983: 34–5).

This last point is interesting, because it is precisely a perceived challenge to political power organized at the level of the nation-state, brought about in part by the technicalities and application of digital communication technologies, that is at the heart of accounts of the politics of the network society. By these accounts, the organization of political authority and activity at the level of the sovereign national state, and the political practices structured by this organization, are in the midst of a crisis which is giving birth to new, competing forms of political organization and practice. This perceived crisis arises from the dynamics discussed in chapters 1 and 3 under the rubric of globalization. As we have seen, the logic and technologies of networks are closely connected with these dynamics; as we will see, it is also the case that network logic and technologies have been identified as intimately linked with the politics purportedly arising in the wake of this crisis. This chapter will proceed along three paths: an examination of the purported demise of the nation-state as the primary container of political power, organization and practice in the present era; an account of the 'new politics' presented as definitive of the political condition of the network society; and assessment of the democratic prospects of political life in the network society.

Globalization: from nation-state to network

The location of sovereignty in the institutions of the nation-state has, arguably, been the definitive characteristic of modern political organization. Sovereignty, in its classic formation, refers to the holding and exercise of supreme political power, the power to make *judgements* (e.g., about the distribution of collective resources or the regulation of individual behaviour) that are binding on others and the power to *act* (e.g., by applying force or offering inducements) to enforce compliance with those judgements. In short, sovereignty denotes the power to rule. In the history of human political society sovereignty has, of course, been organized in a variety of ways, and vested in a range of bodies – local lords, the Catholic Church, and emperors of various persuasions, to name but a few examples. The assumption of sovereignty by states is generally thought to have originated in Europe in 1648, with the Treaty of Westphalia, which ended the Thirty Years' War, diminished the authority of the Church and established the normative principles upon which the modern system of states would eventually be based: 'territorial sovereignty, the formal equality of states, non-intervention in the internal affairs of other recognized states, and state consent as the foundation stone of international legal agreement . . .' (Held and McGrew 2002: 11). These principles would eventually be embodied in the nation-states that emerged in western Europe in the eighteenth and nineteenth centuries and, through processes of decolonization, imperial dissolution and emulation, would come to occupy nearly the entire surface of the globe by the late twentieth century.

Indeed, the territorial organization of sovereignty is central to Max Weber's classic definition of the state as 'a human community that claims a monopoly on the legitimate use of force over a given territory and people'. Here, the legitimate (i.e., legally authorized – all sorts of actors within a society use force, only the state and its delegates can do so legitimately) use of coercive force is understood as the ultimate, though certainly not the only, expression of sovereign power. The state is the entity that has *jurisdiction* over activity within a given territory, including the exclusive right to act coercively, if alternative means of socialization, persuasion or inducement fail, to enforce that jurisdiction. It is the security of this ultimate power that guarantees the state's sovereign authority on all matters within its territory. The action of the state is not limited to force (indeed, it is generally supposed that the relative absence of coercion is the best indicator of the stability, legitimacy and security of state sovereignty) but it is the prospect of resort to ultimate force if need be that finally underwrites all the other judgements and actions the state undertakes. States engage in all sorts of actions, including, for example, the redistribution of public and private resources, but the action which defines a state in distinction to other political actors and institutions is its ultimate, exclusive, ability to act with legally sanctioned coercive measures to put its judgements into effect in the event they are opposed.

That a state enjoys a *monopoly* on the legitimate use of force *within its territory* is crucial, because it is this combination of monopoly and a fixed boundary that generates the exclusivities that define the sovereign authority of the state. That is to say, the state is sovereign when it enjoys *exclusive*, ultimate authority over matters within its borders. This means that there can be no other actor or body internal to its boundaries (e.g., a citizens' militia) that challenges the completeness of the state's sovereignty by also claiming the right to use force (or legislate, or tax, or regulate, or any of the other activities that flow from the state's coercive power) when it sees fit, without the authorization of the state. It also means that there can be no actor or body external to its boundaries (e.g., another state) that claims the right to exercise coercive authority within the state's territory, contrary to the state's wishes. When an internal competitor succeeds in challenging the state's ultimate authority within its territory, the state's sovereignty dissolves into civil war or revolution. When an external competitor succeeds in such a challenge, the state's sovereignty has been usurped by war or conquest. When a state succeeds in maintaining ultimate power within its territory against internal and external competitors, the state enjoys the autonomy and self-determination that accrue to sovereignty. As David Held and Anthony McGrew point out, the particularity of the modern state lies in its embodiment of a 'distinctive symmetry and correspondence between sovereignty, territory and legitimacy' (Held and McGrew 2002: 10).

Within a nation-state, sovereignty can be organized in a number of ways, and vested in a variety of institutions. Initially, the sovereignty of nation-states was vested in the persons of absolute monarchs. Monarchies persist but, with few exceptions, their relationship to sovereign political authority is largely formal. Since the liberal revolutions of the seventeenth and eighteenth centuries in Europe and America, the power of national monarchies has progressively diminished, and sovereignty has been reconstituted in the depersonalized institutions we have come to associate most closely with the modern nation-state. Today, the ostensible vessels of state sovereignty include written constitutions and statutes, the executive, legislative and judicial branches of government, the police and military, and bureaucratic state agencies. In liberal democratic societies, the legitimacy of sovereign power, as embodied in these institutions, is founded upon its authorization via the consent of the citizens over whom it is exercised. The precise character of, and relationships between these institutions have varied from one nation-state to the next, and some states – those we designate as 'federal' rather than 'unitary' – even disaggregate sovereignty into subterritorial units within the boundaries of their national territory. Nevertheless, the basic organization of depersonalized sovereignty in institutions contained by national boundaries is relatively standard. It is this configuration that has, by and large, characterized the organization of political authority in the modern world.

Why did sovereignty congeal in specifically *national* units in the modern period? The complete answer to this question is complex, and well beyond the parameters of our investigation here. One part of the answer, however, is that through the period in which sovereign authority was being reorganized, economic activity – markets and trade – also constituted itself in national (i.e., larger than local or regional) units across Europe. National states developed, at least in part, as the logical scale of organization for the exercise of sovereign authority in the regulation of economic activity – the enforcement of contracts, the establishment of common currencies, the protection of markets, etc. It would be an oversimplification to suggest that the development of national economies 'produced' nation-states, but it is the case that the organization of sovereign political power in national units occurred alongside the distinctly modern organization of various aspects of social and economic life into national units as well. The national organization of political authority in the institutions of the nation-state thus reflects, and reinforces, the national organization of social and economic life. Politics, in this complex, is understood to comprise that range of activities in which a variety of civic actors compete (or cooperate) to determine or influence the application of the state's sovereign powers of judgement and action, and in which states interact with each other in the international arena. This 'state-centric' understanding of politics has, quite justifiably, been criticized as overly narrow, insofar as it fails to recognize that politics – social practices of judgement and action, and the exertion of power – are present at sites that have little direct relation to the institutionalized sovereign authority of the nation-state. In this broader sense, politics exists in every human relationship. That being said, the dominant meanings attached to 'politics' in the modern period clearly identify this word with the competition to control the institutionalized, sovereign power of the nation-state, and the governments that carry that power.

It is also important to note that distinctly modern communication technologies, such as the printing press, telegraph, and radio and television broadcasting, have been instrumental to the organization of social and economic activity, and certainly to the exertion and maintenance of sovereign political authority, on a national scale. In the case of the latter, it was these technologies that made possible the more or less simultaneous, standardized communication of political authority from a centralized state apparatus to a national public dispersed across a national territory; it was also these technologies that made it possible for those centralized authorities to receive information about compliance or threats (both internal and external), to which they could then more or less rapidly respond (Innis 1950). Mass media technologies such as the press and broadcasting have also been singled out as instrumental to the formation, maintenance and shape of national public spheres, the political arenas of civil society in which liberal democratic citizenship is enacted, public opinion is formed, and the legitimacy of sovereign state authority is tested (Habermas 1989).

It is this constellation that has, purportedly, been recently disturbed, resulting in what has been described as a trans-formation to a distinctly *post*modern geopolitical formation, in which the nation-state as the autonomous agency of sov-ereign political power has been 'unbundled' (Deibert 1997: 138; Elkins 1995; Ruggie 1993). In response to the dynam-ics of globalization, the independent, sovereign power of the state is said to have declined precipitously. Globalization, of course, admits of multiple meanings and consists in many aspects. In relation to the status of political authority orga-nized and exercised at the level of the nation-state, however, its meaning is fairly precise: the capacity of states to exercise exclusively the ultimate power of judgement and action within their territories has been decisively diminished. In other words, sovereignty has become unbundled, as states no longer enjoy the exclusive power to prescribe and proscribe activity within their national jurisdictions. This power is now shared amongst a constellation of domestic and international public and private actors and institutions, ranging from private, transnational corporations to an increasing array of international policy-making venues, including the IMF, the WTO, the G7, the European Union, Asia-Pacific Economic Cooperation and Mercosur, to name but a few. As Held and McGrew observe, 'National government is increasingly locked into an array of global, regional and multilayered systems of governance – and can barely monitor it all, let alone stay in command' (Held and McGrew 2002: 19).

The roots of the state's apparent crisis of sovereignty lie in the dynamics of deterritorialization, some aspects of which have been discussed in earlier chapters. Put simply, the logic and effectiveness of organizing sovereignty at the national level, and investing it exclusively in nation-states, was premised on a corresponding organization of primary social and economic activities within national containers. However, as the twentieth century gave way to the twenty-first, a good deal of social and economic activity was being prosecuted across, rather than within, national boundaries, and so

nationally organized political authority no longer corres-
ponded with the prevailing spatial orientations of economy
and society. It is in this tension that the challenge to the sovereignty and autonomy of nation-states becomes manifest.

As discussed in chapter 2, the dynamic of globalization is
most evident in the deterritorialization and transnationalization of economic activity from the 1980s onwards. No
modern economy was ever completely sealed within its
national territory, and states have always allowed and
engaged in trade and commerce across borders. Nevertheless,
an *inter*national economy in which nationally contained economic actors interact with one another is not the same as an
economy in which economic actors and activities are themselves organized *trans*nationally. At a certain point the sheer
quantity of economic activity – trade, production, financial
speculation, currency exchange, foreign investment and consumption – taking place across national borders increased
to a level at which it became a *qualitative* change, and it
was no longer possible to describe modern economies as
'organized, planned, measured, and thus overwhelmingly
contained within discrete sovereign-territorial boundaries'
(Deibert 1997: 138). A number of factors stimulated this
process of economic deterritorialization, including increased
international migration, and significant advances in transportation and communication technology. But perhaps chief
among these enabling factors was the more or less voluntary
decision by prosperous states to ease limits the exercise of
their independent sovereign authority might otherwise place
on economic enterprise and accumulation within the free
market.

This consensus has been codified in a string of bilateral
and multilateral economic covenants, including global agreements such as the General Agreement on Tariffs and Trade
and the General Agreement on Trade in Services, and a
variety of similar regional accords, such as the North American Free Trade Agreement and the treaties of the European
Union. Together, these accords comprise the constitution of
the global economy and, by extension, establish the parameters within which states can exercise their sovereign political
authority. At a most basic level, what they require is that
states treat foreign goods, capital and enterprises as they

would their own, thus removing from the state's arsenal, in most cases, instruments such as tariffs and other trade barriers, subsidies, targeted tax concessions, foreign ownership and investment limits, and other forms of prejudicial treatment aimed at protecting and supporting domestic firms or meeting non-market national interests and priorities. Violation can invoke retaliatory measures by other states, suits against the offending state by the offended private party, or sanctions levelled by the international tribunals charged with resolving disputes under these agreements. In sum, states have pledged to liberate the flow of economic activity (i.e., goods, capital, currency, services) by restricting their own ability to regulate those flows independently in response to domestic pressures or priorities that might not be encompassed by the desire for economic growth. In this way, states have basically ceded a portion of their sovereignty, in the first place to the increasingly powerful transnational economic actors who benefit most from these arrangements and, in the second place, to the nascent international institutions that have been developed to enforce the new constitution of globalization. States, it would seem, no longer enjoy exclusive jurisdiction over what happens within their territory. Interestingly, this parcelling out of the state's sovereignty has been accomplished without the violence of revolution from within, or war from without. Also, states basically retain their monopoly on the legitimate use of force within their territory, even in the midst of what might otherwise be described as a serious undermining of their political autonomy. However, rather than indicating that the state's sovereignty remains unaffected by globalization, these facts serve to cast doubt upon traditional definitions of sovereignty that locate it solely in an unchallenged monopoly on the exercise of legitimate physical coercion.

Just as the nationalization of politics, civil society and citizenship rose in tandem with economic activity and markets structured within national territories, so too has the globalization of the world economy purportedly stimulated a deterritorialization of politics. This is manifested not only in the aforementioned growth of international institutions which enjoy power and jurisdiction without territory, but also in a range of other 'deterritorializations': the disarticulation of territory and identity evident in the rise of international migration and diasporic communities; the heightened awareness and salience of territorially indefinite issues such as human rights and the environment; and the beginnings of a global civil society and possibly even a transnational/ deterritorialized public sphere. Of course, intimately linked with each of these is the accelerated deterritorialization of communication, accomplished by the proliferation of digital technologies that enable multimedia transmission across borders and territorial expanses with considerable efficiency (Deibert 1997).

The complex described above is seen by many as responsible for the democratic crisis that is said to characterize the politics of globalization. This crisis operates on two levels: the level of the nation-state; and the level of the international venues to which its power is apparently shifting. On the first level, as outlined above, membership in the global economic marketplace is contingent upon a range of commitments made by states to refrain from intervening prejudicially in the flow of a range of economic values. These economic commitments are also political commitments insofar as they limit states' ability to secure non-market public goods, and to respond when the democratically expressed will of their citizens directs them to do so. Furthermore, the specific commitments entailed in membership in the global market economy are such that, in many cases, they undermine the state's capacity to deliver the benefits of social welfare and security that have been the cornerstone of the state's legitimacy since at least the end of the Second World War. Castells describes the situation as follows:

> The globalization of production and investment also threatens the welfare state, a key element in the policies of the nation-state in the past half-century, and probably the main building block of its legitimacy in industrialized countries . . . In an economy whose core markets for capital, goods and services are increasingly integrated on a global scale, there is little room for vastly different welfare states . . . welfare states are being downsized to the lowest common denominator that keeps spiraling downwards. So doing, a fundamental component of the legitimacy and stability of the nation-state fades away. (Castells 1997: 252–4)

The spirit of the global economy is the spirit of universal market liberalism, which implies minimizing the state's role in using its sovereign authority to redistribute resources according to localized social welfare demands, and a dismantling of the instruments necessary to play this role. In the new global economy, states attend to public welfare by competing with other states to supply market conditions that can attract private investment and enterprise, which liberal orthodoxy insists is the foundation of generalized prosperity. Such market conditions involve as little redistributive and regulatory state intervention as possible. This makes it difficult for the state to deliver the goods of material security that have historically motivated the consent from which liberal democratic states derive their political legitimacy. Under these conditions, it is no longer clear to citizens what their state does or can do for them, or what influence they have over the judgements their state makes, or the actions it takes.

The globalization of politics that follows the globalization of economy contributes to a democratic crisis in a second way, this time in the network of international institutions with which states now effectively share a good portion of their sovereignty. Decisions made by institutions such as the IMF, the WTO, the OECD and the World Bank have a decisive impact upon life in the countries that are subject to them. With few exceptions, however, these bodies lack the institutionalized mechanisms for participation, representation, scrutiny and accountability that are necessary for them to claim democratic legitimacy. In short, the WTO, to take one example, has no citizens. It is true that the membership of these organizations is comprised of representatives of sovereign states who remain accountable to their people via national structures of liberal democratic politics, including elections. Still, there is a widespread perception that such indirect mechanisms are insufficient and incomplete, more accommodating to transnational corporate interests than to everyday citizens, and that these powerful institutions are even more closed and exclusive than the governments of nation-states. The evidence of this perception can be found on the streets of Seattle, Genoa, Prague and Quebec City, in piles of broken window glass and sputtering tear-gas canisters, and in the faces of throngs of coughing, bleary-eyed activists who vent their democratic rage at the chain link fences and riot police that now routinely separate them from their de facto governors. Thus the politics of globalization is often described in terms of a democratic crisis that operates at both national and international levels.

It is important to note that there are many who argue that reports of the demise of the nation-state and its sovereignty are greatly exaggerated. The contours of the debate between those who are sure, and those who have doubts, about the progress of globalization and the decline of the nation-state have been well chronicled elsewhere and will not be reviewed comprehensively here (Held and McGrew 2002). Briefly, those who are sceptical of the breadth and depth of globalization as described above marshal a number of arguments. One holds that what is being described as a new phenomenon is really just the continued progress of an old one, namely the growing economic and political interdependence of nation-states, a process which simply became generalized with the collapse of the Soviet Union and its satellites in the last decade of the twentieth century (Hirst 1997; Rugman 2000). Another suggests that 'globalization' misnames the current situation, either because the unevenness with which its fruits and burdens are distributed across the planet means that the phenomenon of globalization is anything but global, and that many people continue to experience their world as confined by the economic misfortunes of their nation and locality (Hoogvelt 1997), or because what is really going on is 'Americanization' – the extension of American economic, political, military and cultural hegemony throughout the world in the wake of the collapse of its primary competitor (Gilpin 1987). Economists point out that significant 'border effects' continue to contain economies within national territorial, linguistic and cultural boundaries, affording states much more room for political autonomy in relation to economic matters than is supposed in most accounts of globalization (Helliwell 2002). Similarly, realists insist that, regardless of multilateralism and interdependence, there remain no organizations that rival the independent economic and military resources, and so the power, of modern nation-states. Finally, radical critics suggest that globalization is more of an ideological device than a material reality, a discourse generated to obscure the responsibility of states for their commitments to neo-liberal, market capitalism, their abandonment of the welfare state, and their power to reverse these commitments (Callinicos et al. 1994). Here, rhetoric conjuring an impotent postmodern state takes on a performative aspect, becoming a sort of self-fulfilling prophecy: if people believe the state has been incapacitated by globalization, they are less likely to demand that it intercede in the accumulation strategies of private capital on behalf of the common good.

These points are not without merit. Still, the preponderance of evidence seems to suggest that, as Held and McGrew conclude, 'the modern state is increasingly embedded in webs of regional and global interconnectedness permeated by supranational, intergovernmental and transnational forces, unable to determine its own fate' (Held and McGrew 2002: 23). Whatever the case, the account given above of the decline of the nation-state under the pressures of globalization is central to the network society thesis. For Castells, especially, contemporary politics can be understood only in light of the waning of the sovereignty and autonomy of the nation-state. As he puts it, 'State control over space and time is increasingly bypassed by global flows of capital, goods, services, technology, communication and information' (Castells 1997: 243). In regard to the political effects of economic globalization, Castells is quite categorical: 'the nation-state is increasingly powerless in controlling monetary policy, deciding its budget, organizing production and trade, collecting its corporate taxes and fulfilling its commitments to provide social benefits. In sum, it has lost most of its economic power . . .' (Castells 1997: 254). In characteristic fashion, Castells advances the model of the network as both a contributor to, and an outcome of, the state's descent into powerlessness. Thus, the power of states has been usurped by 'networks of capital, production, communication, crime, international institutions, supranational military apparatuses, non-governmental organizations, transnational religions and public opinion movements', and the upshot of this reorganization is that 'while nation-states continue to exist, and they will continue to do so in the foreseeable future, they are, and they will increasingly be, *nodes of a broader network of power*' (Castells 1997: 304; emphasis original). In a context where the nation-state represented ultimate sovereign power, politics quite naturally concentrated on winning control of the state apparatus; when the nation-state is reduced to a node in a complex network, gaining control of its apparatus 'becomes just one means among others to assert power' (Castells 1997: 305). If this is correct – and it is not an uncontroversial position – then politics in the network society is unlikely to look very much like politics as usual.

New media, new politics

As discussed above, one of the political outcomes of globalization has been what is perceived as a growing crisis in liberal democracy, in which citizens find that the states in relation to which they enjoy citizenship are increasingly ineffective, and that the transnational institutions which do hold effective power make little provision for democratic citizenship. In response to this, progressive theorists have made the case, and developed models, for a global political order based on cosmopolitan democratic governance and citizenship, but, despite their persuasiveness, these visions have yet to be institutionalized comprehensively (Archibugi et al. 1998; Held 1995; Hutchings and Dannreuther 1999). The challenges to democracy posed by globalization have been compounded by, or perhaps reflected in, a widely diagnosed democratic malaise afflicting most Western countries, in which citizens have become increasingly alienated from, and distrustful of, formal processes and institutions of democratic participation, including voting for representatives in elections and supporting established political parties.

It is from the wreckage caused by the democratic crisis of old politics that the new politics of the network society supposedly emerges (Webster 2001). Castells describes this new politics as 'informational politics' and connects it directly to network communication technologies. As he puts it:

> The key point is that electronic media (including not only television and radio, but all forms of communication, such as

newspapers and the Internet) have become the privileged space of politics. Not that all politics can be reduced to images, sounds or symbolic manipulation. But, without it, there is no chance of winning or exercising power... [B]ecause of the convergent effects of traditional political systems and of dramatically increased pervasiveness of the new media, political communication and information are essentially captured in the space of media. Outside the media sphere there is only political marginality. (Castells 1997: 311–12)

Politics, according to Castells, has been 'capture[d] in the space of the media' and the inability of traditional political actors and institutions to adapt successfully to 'informational politics' is a 'fundamental source of the crisis of democracy in the Information Age' (Castells 1997: 312). In his estimation, 'because current political systems are still based in organizational forms and political strategies of the industrial era, they have become politically obsolete, and their autonomy is being denied by the flows of information on which they depend' (Castells 1997: 312).

The new politics is thus a politics of struggling over information management and control in the 'space' constructed by prevailing media of communication, as a necessary precondition of access to more material forms of power. Politics, in this view, is a contest to define the parameters of public discourse, and the symbolic and cultural codes through which norms and expectations are expressed and circulated. This means that a *minimum* condition of political action is access to, and presence and/or representation within, the arenas (i.e., mass communication media) in which these battles are engaged. It is for this reason that those who are systematically denied access to advanced information and communication media, or whose access to them is limited to passive consumption of commodified content, are not only economically disadvantaged in the network society, but also politically disenfranchised. The digital divide is, consequently, at once a technological, economic and political divide, a divide which sets the terms of access to citizenship itself, both within technologically developed regions and between wealthy and impoverished areas in the global system.

Beyond this minimum, really effective, influential political agency now requires facility with complex modalities, techniques and technologies of symbolic mobilization and political communication. Politics in this context is less a practice of public judgement and action than it is a profession of public relations, trading in the complex crafting and circulation of highly coded 'messages' using sophisticated technologies of information gathering and dissemination. Historically, access to these resources has been unequally distributed. Democracy has always centred on the politics of persuasion, and politics understood as the manipulation of public discourse is rooted deep in the ancient origins of this form of government, wherein power required possession of the skills of persuasive rhetoric, and professionals willing to hire out their expertise in this area were highly influential. Today, the ability to shape and move public discourse through communication remains crucial to the exercise of power and influence, though the *polis* has given way to the 24-hour TV news channel, and the sophists of Athens have been replaced by pollsters, image consultants, pundits, spin doctors, database engineers, public relations teams and advertising experts armed with market-tested catchphrases, media strategies, website designs and demographic profiles. In this sense, the informational politics of the network society simply escalates tendencies that have always been present, wherever political power has been organized via institutions that are at least formally democratic.

The character of the 'new politics', and the role that new information and communication technologies play in relation to it, can be profitably discussed in relation to the politics of globalization. According to the model of informational politics, the political contest over globalization is best understood as an instance of the politics of signification, a struggle over the cultural codes through which the sign 'globalization' enters and circulates in public discourse, a struggle over meaning. Does/will globalization mean extension of the rights and freedoms associated with liberal democracy, a sharing of the prosperity associated with market capitalism, rising standards of living, enhanced intercultural understanding and harmony, international peace, solidarity and global democracy? Or does/will it mean the end of national self-determination and autonomy, the triumph of unaccountable transnational corporations and institutions over democratic governments, global dominance of American cultural commodities, a deepening of the dependency and exploitation of the developing world, environmental degradation and an assault on working people? The first set of meanings is the one preferred by the forces of transnational capital that stand to gain most from globalization on the neo-liberal model; the second set is preferred by the multifaceted transnational social movement that has risen in opposition to these forces. Which will ultimately settle in as definitive in popular discourse and the public imagination depends, in the paradigm being discussed here, on the outcome of an ongoing struggle over cultural definition that is being waged in the global circuits of mediated communication. Who will succeed in branding globalization? This is the informational politics of the network society.

Network technologies provide resources to both sides in this contest. The importance of these technologies to the forces of transnational capital has been detailed above and in chapter 3. Network technologies provide the infrastructure for the various economic flows of transnational capitalism, and their deterritorializing effects undermine the ability of national governments, democratically accountable to the public interest, to impose limits on these powerful economic actors. Network technologies have also provided an opportunity and means for transnational elites to consolidate their control over the global mediascape, through a dramatic concentration of ownership, through horizontal and vertical integration, across media-platforms, and across the content/carriage divide (Compaine and Gomery 2000; McChesney 1999; D. Schiller 1999). Fewer and fewer transnational conglomerates control more and more of the infrastructure and content of global communication networks, and these conglomerates are intricately nested with the corporate interests of the rest of the global capitalist economy, both at the level of ownership as well as in their dependency on commercial advertising (Herman and McChesney 1997). It is not without reason that the liberalization of global telecommunication markets was, in many ways, the crucial leading edge of the globalization wedge. The mania of global media convergence that characterized the late 1990s seems to have reached the limits of its profitability in the early years of the twenty-first century, but this does diminish the role that digital technologies have played in enhancing the hold enjoyed by transnational capital on the global cultural and consciousness industries (Croteau and Hoynes 2001). This, of course, confers considerable advantage upon those in whose political interest it is to define globalization in positive terms.

So, too, do digital networks introduce possibilities for the other side in the cultural struggle over the meaning of globalization. Indeed, the rise to prominence of transnational 'new social movements' linked in global civil society networks has relied heavily on the proliferation of network communication technologies, and has been identified as fundamental to the political dynamics of the network society (Castells 1997: 68–109; Deibert 1997: 157–64). The term 'new social movements' captures a broad range of political activity, ideologies and priorities, but it is typically meant to indicate oppositional political formations not encompassed by institutionalized political parties, business associations, trade unions, mainstream interest groups and non-governmental organizations (Dalton and Kuechler 1990; Tarrow 1998). Many new social movements are nationally specific – the Zapatistas in Chiapas, Mexico, the Revolutionary Association of Women of Afghanistan, and the 'patriotic' right-wing militias in the United States, to name but a few prominent examples – and these have made significant use of networked communication technologies to considerable impact within and beyond their respective borders. However, it is the specifically transnational new social movements whose rise and activity are more strongly identified as definitive of the politics of the network society, largely because these movements are themselves structured as networks. Among these we might include a range of global peace, human rights, social justice, environmental, and women's movements – dynamic, deterritorialized coalitions of local, national and international groups, each of which represents a node in a complex network of flows whose coordination relies heavily on the communication made possible by digital networks (McCaughey and Ayers 2003).

The opportunities afforded to new social movements by digital information and communication networks are considerable. These instruments – especially the applications of e-mail and multimedia, hypertextual websites – provide spatially dispersed activist coalitions with the means to accomplish a range of functions that are central to their operations and impact. In no particular order, these include:

- collection, production, archiving and global publication of information resources (especially political material that might not otherwise be disseminated so widely and inexpensively);
- a platform for event promotion, recruitment, fundraising and the solicitation of other forms of support;
- a delivery system for consciousness raising, political education and training (e.g., instruction in non-violent direct action);
- a means of establishing and maintaining communication links with sympathetic and allied organizations, and the networks of which they are a part;
- a communication system for internal organization, administration, mobilization (e.g., 'action alerts') and coordination of activities;
- a communication system for democratic dialogue, debate and deliberation, contributing to the possibility of a global, democratic public sphere;
- a medium for political communication otherwise prohibited by repressive states;
- a distribution system for independent media, news reporting and alternative journalism that bypasses corporate-controlled mass media;
- an instrument for engagement in novel forms of direct political action (e.g., 'hacktivism', mass e-mail campaigns, denial of service attacks, electronic petitions, website defacement, parody sites, etc.).

The use of digital networks by new social movements in some or all of the ways listed above has been well documented in a growing case-study literature that details how specific movements have made particular uses of these technologies in their activist endeavours (McCaughey and Ayers 2003;

Pendakur and Harris 2002; Webster 2001). Several studies in this literature also point out the limitations and challenges that high-technology organization and activism present to new social movements, including the technological, financial and time/labour resources required to mount and maintain an effective 'digital' movement, issues of privacy and surveillance, over-reliance on a technology to which access is far from equally distributed, vulnerability to technology failure, and issues of censorship/freedom of expression, to name but a few. By and large, however, there is a consensus that digital networks have done more to help than to harm the proliferation and effectiveness of new social movements and the global civil society networks into which they coalesce.

This has certainly been the case for those movements involved in the cultural struggle to define the discourse surrounding globalization. The anti-globalization movement is, arguably, the paradigmatic example of a deterritorialized, transnational social movement that has used network technology to organize and execute a campaign of political action aimed at intervening in the corporate construction of cultural meaning – in this case, the meaning of capitalist globalization on the neo-liberal model. Emblematic in this regard was the use of the internet by activists opposed to the Multilateral Agreement on Investment (MAI) negotiated by the OECD in the late 1990s (Deibert 2002; Potter 2002; Smith and Smythe 2001). Had it been adopted, the MAI would have pledged signatories to relax national controls on foreign investment that prejudicially benefited domestic interests, and it would have made provision for private corporations to sue states that violated this pledge. A wide variety of international groups saw in the MAI a dramatic diminution of the sovereign authority of national governments and the citizens to which they are accountable, as well as an equally dramatic escalation in the power of transnational capital. According to Deibert:

> MAI detractors include a wide array of different interest groups – as many as 600 non-governmental organizations from at least seventy countries by some estimates – in areas such as the environment, labour, and culture, each with its own set of sectoral criticisms. Common objections, however,

centre on several key themes, at the forefront of which is the
issue of diminished state sovereignty and growing corporate
power and rights. (Deibert 2002: 92–3)

These groups would eventually coalesce into a global
network whose activity culminated in the violent police
repression of massive anti-MAI demonstrations at the 1999
meetings of the WTO in Seattle, and the (temporary) collapse
of the agreement.

Most analysts see the anti-MAI campaign as a foundational moment in the development of the international anti-
globalization movement, and point to the crucial role played
in its development by network organization and new information and communication technologies, in particular the
internet. Electronic mailing-lists and websites were used
extensively to share information amongst activists; to provide
forums for debate and discussion of issues, critiques and
strategy; to develop, circulate and coordinate plans for
collective action, including the Seattle protests; to educate
activists in civil disobedience tactics; to publicize information,
including drafts of the agreement, analysis and commentary;
to provide a source of independent, alternative media information; and to engage in direct action placing pressure on
government officials and agencies (Deibert 2002; Potter
2002; Smith and Smythe 2001). As Smith and Smythe
suggest, 'In essence, the Internet helped to break the information monopoly enjoyed by business, government leaders,
and OECD officials' (Smith and Smythe 2001: 200). In a
context in which politics is understood as a struggle to
control cultural codes, discourse and meaning, the significance of this development should not be underestimated.
Neither should it be overestimated, however. Few would deny
that network technology was, and continues to be, an important enabler of the transnational network of new social movements that carries the anti-globalization campaign, and that
the successes of this campaign have been felt in recent
gestures by international institutions towards increased transparency and engagement with 'civil society' in their decision-
making procedures. Still, it would be misleading to suggest
that network technology 'created' the anti-globalization
movement, that the internet was responsible for the collapse

of the MAI, or that the impact upon broader public opinion of the network-coordinated protests that are now routinely visited upon meetings of the agencies of capitalist globalization has been unambiguously positive (Potter 2002: 96–104).

This raises the question of whether it pays to think of the politics of the network society as decisively 'new'. It is certainly the case that a diverse array of social movements, many of them deterritorialized in both their organization and their concerns, have risen to prominence in recent years, and they have found a remarkable tool in networked information and communication technologies, a tool which enables and, in many cases, amplifies their political voice. Yet, it bears keeping mind that the political uses of network technology described above, so significant to new social movements as well as to more traditional political actors, represent only a minor portion of the uses to which these technologies are put by most of the people who use them on a daily basis.

Even in countries where access to network technologies is relatively widespread, distinctly political uses of these instruments are the exception, rather than the norm. Use patterns among internet users in the European Union in 2000, for example, reveal that 69% of users exchange e-mail with friends, family and work colleagues, 47% take part in online training and education, 47% make searches for product information, 43% get free software downloads, 38% make searches for sports and recreational information, 28% are involved in gaming and 23% make job searches. These and other distinctly non-political uses all far outrank even relatively minimal, mainstream, pedestrian political uses such as visiting government (15%) and political party websites (10%) (Norris 2001: 225). Recent studies of use patterns in North America have yielded similar results (Barney 2003: 114). One can only imagine that more demanding and marginal political uses such as those characteristic of the vigorous politics of new social movements would rank even lower. Indeed, only 10% of regular internet users in the European Union even indicated an interest in using the internet for the purpose of contacting a politician or engaging in political debate (Norris 2001: 223). A similar picture emerges from consideration of the types of sites internet users typically search for and visit on the world wide web. As Dordoy and Mellor report: 'Of the top twenty search terms for April 2000, seven were sex-related, three chat or Hotmail, five computer music or games related. *No search term that might relate to political discourse appears in the top 100*' (Dordoy and Mellor, 2001: 175; emphasis added). What this suggests is that the internet serves primarily to reinforce existing patterns of political engagement and participation, rather than to engage a new citizenry and mobilize a new politics. Pippa Norris expresses this dynamic of reinforcement as follows:

> through repeated [internet] use the most politically engaged will be reinforced in their civic activism. In contrast . . . the most politically disengaged will be largely immunized from political messages on the Net . . . If this interpretation is correct and if this situation persists as Internet use spreads and normalizes, it suggests that there will be a growing 'democratic divide' in civic involvement. Far from mobilizing the general public, the Internet may thereby function to increase divisions between the actives and apathetics within societies . . . it is difficult to know how the Internet *per se* can ever reach the civically disengaged. (Norris 2001: 230–1)

Network technologies provide formidable tools with which the stubborn minority of politically engaged citizens in Western liberal democracies can carry out, and perhaps even amplify, their efforts; these same technologies also provide the tools with which the as-stubbornly-depoliticized majority can pursue their continued disengagement from political life. It is difficult to see what is particularly 'new' in this configuration, besides the tools with which it is maintained.

Thus, new instruments do not necessarily make for new politics, but the claim that the politics of the network society is 'new' rests not only on an account of the character of the instruments political actors use, but also on certain assumptions about the object of political action, and the organization of political power. On these grounds too, I believe, we have reason to question the 'new politics' thesis. To say that politics is *primarily* informational, and that power is gathered and wielded in communicative practices of cultural codification, symbolic manipulation and discourse management is a contestable claim. From the perspective of many people in the world, in both wealthy and poor countries, the source and instruments of power remain material wealth and physical force – the dollar and the gun – and politics remains the struggle to control these, a struggle in which control over discourse and cultural meaning is important, but still secondary. Consider the following passage from Castells:

> Cultural battles are the power battles of the Information Age. They are primarily fought in and by the media, but the media are not the power-holders. Power, as the capacity to impose behaviour, lies in the network of information exchange and symbolic manipulation, which relate social actors, institutions, and cultural movements, through icons, spokespersons and intellectual amplifiers. In the long run, it does not really matter who is in power because the distribution of political roles becomes widespread and rotating. There are no more stable power elites. (Castells 1998: 368)

One would be hard pressed to convince, for example, aboriginal peoples in Canada, or women in Afghanistan – both of whom have made inventive and effective uses of information technology and who have engaged creatively in the cultural politics of meaning – that 'it does not really matter who is in power' and that there are no more stable power elites. Their struggles are cultural, to be sure, but not just cultural, and perhaps not even primarily so. Here, it would seem, we reach the limit of the network model for understanding politics, even in a world in which network technologies are mediating important changes. In these cases, and in too many other similar ones, the sort of power that matters is not diffused in 'networks of information exchange and symbolic manipulation', it is, rather, concentrated in the hands of the state, and wielded by the economic and military elites who control the instruments of its sovereign judgement and action, and whose advantage is more entrenched than 'rotating', even in nominal democracies. The same might be said of the war against Iraq in 2003, in which a deterritorialized social movement, using sophisticated network technologies to mobilize and organize its opposition, was quite unable to affect the exercise of the sovereign power of the nation-states of the USA, the United Kingdom and Australia (to name only three) in securing the region in accordance with their interests. Such power, a very old and enduring sort of power, is exercised in ways that are somewhat more concrete than symbolic, and it is neither easily escaped nor effectively opposed by the use of network technology.

Network technologies and democracy

Setting aside the question of whether the network society can be characterized as animated by a politics that is fundamentally new, it is also important to consider the possibilities network technologies present for the old politics which, at least in some parts of the world, are by and large the politics of liberal democracy organized at the national level. As is well known, the arrival of new information and communication technologies was attended by an often euphoric discourse that these would be the instruments of a radical democratic renaissance, and this discourse has proved to be quite persistent. As Castells observes, 'The Internet was expected to be an ideal instrument to further democracy – and it still is' (Castells 2001: 155). One of our deepest liberal democratic intuitions is that generalized advance in our ability to gather and share information, and to communicate with one another, invigorates democratic politics. Information and communication, we believe, are foundational to democracy, and therefore technologies that expand our access to these must contribute positively to democracy's achievement and enhancement. The internet, which provides relatively widespread, instant access to increasing volumes of politically relevant information, and which enables direct, undistorted communication between citizens, and between citizens and their rulers, simply must be such a technology.

On the face of it, this is not an unreasonable expectation. Democracy, in whatever form it exists, is a deeply communicative brand of politics. It demands the communication and exchange of information and views. It demands dialogue, and a public sphere, in which citizens can engage in the practices that define them as citizens and their society as democratic: the dissemination of information; the expression and consideration of contending viewpoints; rational, critical debate on issues of common concern; scrutiny of public authority and policy; the presentation and contestation of reasons; the holding of officials to account. In small-scale political organizations, the public sphere emerges in face-to-face public communication. In large-scale political units, such as our modern cities, provinces and nation-states, the democratic public sphere, to the extent it exists at all, exists primarily by virtue of its mediation by mass information and communication technologies: the printed word; the photograph; the radio; the cinema; the television; and now, we suppose, the internet.

However, the relationship between mass communication technologies and democracy has never been this simple. As Bruce Bimber points out, our intuitions are belied by the history of the growth of mass information and communication media in the twentieth century. For, despite a dramatic trajectory of technological expansion in information and communication capacity, democratic participation has not improved significantly in quantitative or qualitative terms over this period. As Bimber writes, in an article documenting the absence of statistical evidence linking internet use independently to increased political engagement (in its various forms) in the United States:

> Opportunities to become better informed have apparently expanded historically, as the informational context of politics has grown richer and become better endowed with media and ready access to political communication. Yet none of the major developments in communication in the 20th Century produced any aggregate gain in citizen participation. Neither telephones, radio, nor television exerted a net positive effect on participation, despite the fact that they apparently reduced information costs and improved citizens' access to information. (Bimber 2001: 57)

Still, expectations that the internet will reverse this trend remain high. And it could be argued that the internet will succeed where previous media of mass communication have failed, precisely because its technical attributes – specifically its decentralized architecture and interactive applications – enable practices that centralized, one-way broadcast media such as the mass press, radio and TV do not. The internet, after all, is not just any old information and communication technology.

There are, to be sure, many reasons to be hopeful that these technologies could contribute to a political life that is more informed, more participatory, more engaged, more inclusive, more responsive, more egalitarian – in a word, more democratic. Among the possible contributions the new technologies might make to an enhanced democratic politics, we might list the following:

* more *convenient, generalized access to a massive volume of politically relevant information*, including information produced by and about government and its critics;
* a medium for *publication*, by a plurality of sources, of a broader diversity of public-interest information than is characteristic of highly centralized, corporate-controlled, commercial mass media;
* a powerful, relatively accessible tool of *organization, mobilization and action* for politically active individuals, groups and organizations;
* a means of *enhanced, routine, vertical communication* between citizens and legislators/officials, enabling improved representation, responsiveness and scrutiny, and heightened accountability;
* a medium of *enhanced horizontal communication* amongst citizens, including expanded opportunities for *public dialogue and deliberation* on issues of common concern;
* a mechanism to enable more *direct forms of popular participation in democratic decision-making*, such as online voting, and deliberative opinion polling;
* an infrastructure for the erection and maintenance of *a more inclusive, politicized public sphere* than that mediated by existing, commercial mass media.

This is a formidable set of potentials, and network technologies certainly provide the technical capacity to make good on each of them. It is also the case that many of these have materialized, to varying degrees, in actual political practices, in a variety of contexts, and have inspired creative experimentation (Agre and Schuler 1997; Becker and Slaton 2000; Schuler

1996; Tsagarousianou et al. 1998). There is no reason to reflexively dismiss the possibility that network technologies might make a significant, enduring contribution to the enhancement of actually existing democratic practice.

On the other hand, there are also substantial reasons to believe that these particular potentials will not be realized, and that network technologies might just as well serve to reinforce the undemocratic tendencies of contemporary mainstream politics, and perhaps even to undermine the possibility of their transformation in democratic directions. For example, as has been noted often in the foregoing pages, new information and communication technologies have also been intimately involved in a dramatic consolidation of the power, and extension of the reach, of existing, global, corporate mass media. The grip on global circuits of mass communication and consciousness exerted by massive, transnational, commercial media conglomerates has been strengthened, rather than weakened, in the age of network technology (McChesney 1999). We also know that, among the relatively small number of people who use the internet to seek political information, the vast majority of these do so by visiting the sites of established mass information providers – CNN, major national newspapers, the BBC, etc. (Norris 2001: 218–19). This suggests that the potential for the internet to deliver a diverse plurality of alternative political information is unlikely to be realized, on a widespread basis, very soon, despite the fact that an unprecedented volume of exactly this sort of information is in fact conveniently available via this medium.

There is also little evidence to suggest that network technologies are being used to facilitate a systematic democratization of the practices of governance and representation in the primary institutions of liberal democratic politics. Governments have been quick to adopt network technologies in order to realize efficiencies in the areas of information access and service delivery. For the most part, however, they have not been as enthusiastic or creative in their deployment of these technologies in order to enhance democratic, public participation in policy- and decision-making. An OECD study of eight leading industrialized countries in 1999 concluded that despite gains in electronic access to information and service delivery, the overall impact of use of the internet by governments has failed to increase access to policy-makers, to improve the transparency of government decision-making, or to facilitate public participation in policy-making (OECD 1999). These findings were confirmed in Norris's comprehensive examination of worldwide trends in 'e-government', which included empirical analysis of the web-sites of nearly 3,000 government departments worldwide, as well as those of 125 legislative chambers in 82 countries. Her findings were instructive: 'Government websites rarely facilitate unmoderated public feedback, few publish public reactions to policy proposals, or used discussion forums, listservs and bulletin boards, although there have been occasional experiments with interactive formats' (Norris 2001: 130). Similar international studies confirm what amounts to a general trend: the rapid adoption of network technology by governments the world over for the purposes of more efficient information access and service delivery, but relatively little serious effort at using these technolo-gies to transform practices of decision- and policy-making (Coleman et al. 1999). This suggests that, in relation to the prospects of enhanced democracy, the impact of network technologies upon governance has been more conservative than transformative.

However, the network *model* has figured into the processes and practices of government in ways that do represent a potentially significant shift – the rise of so-called 'networked governance' (Reinecke 1999). Networked governance refers to the distribution of select government functions into multi-sectoral networks that cross the territorial, jurisdictional and sectoral boundaries that traditionally have served to organize these functions. Under this model, state agencies, private sector actors, and non-governmental, civil society organiza-tions are nodes in networks that accomplish governance in forms that include policy consultation and development, knowledge generation and dissemination, service delivery, the regulation of standards, and programme implementation. In many cases, these networks form temporarily around specific issues or projects, and distribute risk and responsi-bility horizontally, rather than concentrating authority at the top of institutional hierarchies. As such, networked gover-nance is considered by many to be a form perfectly adapted to the dynamic conditions of globalization and technological innovation:

> Networks enable governments to better manage the risks and take advantage of the opportunities that economic liberalization and technological change bring . . . They represent a promising medium through which states and their international organizations can achieve their mission, maintain their competence in a changing global environment, and serve their citizens in a more effective and legitimate way. (Witte et al. 2002: 24)

Here, it is contended that networked governance is more efficient, more inclusive and more flexible than governance monopolized by centralized, hierarchical state institutions, and better able to optimize knowledge-sharing, decision-making, consensus-building and action in response to changing conditions in diverse situations. The Global Public Policy Network, part of the UN's Vision Project, details several international examples of the model of networked governance in action, ranging from the global campaign to ban land mines to the development of a World Commission on Dams (Global Public Policy Network 2003). The network model certainly holds promise for a decentralization and democratization of governance, but it would be an exaggeration to say that this model has replaced the hierarchical, bureaucratic organization of institutional political authority and power, or that it is necessarily democratic in either intention or outcome. It could be argued for example, that networked governance represents, variously: a significant incursion of private interests into public governance; the reorganization of public sector government along corporate lines; a strategy for co-opting civil society opposition without significant devolution of power; and a style of public management freed from traditional structures of democratic representation and accountability. The network model – like network technologies – remains as open to undemocratic possibilities as it is to democratic ones.

What about the ways in which established political parties use networks? In liberal democracies, parties exist primarily to organize the vote in the election of representatives and governments, but they have also traditionally served the functions of educating, aggregating and articulating public opinion, as well as incubating public policy. Historically, parties have been a significant site of democratic participation and citizenship. Parties continue to play these roles, to varying degrees in different contexts, but their status has changed radically with the rise of mass media and public relations, and the 'professionalization' of politics – which have, in many cases, reduced political parties to a combination of fundraising machines and brand names, mobilized during electoral contests but dormant in between. The 'new politics' thesis suggests that political parties are among those traditional institutions that have become thoroughly discredited and increasingly irrelevant to the politics of the network society. Others, however, point to the enduring role of parties in organizing electorates and governments, and suggest that network technologies have the potential to revitalize the democratic function of parties as vehicles for the generation of public opinion and policy.

Parties in affluent liberal democracies have indeed embraced new information and communication technologies (Norris 2001: 148–58). In most cases, parties use these technologies in exactly the same way that new social movements do – e-mail and websites are deployed as instruments of publication, recruitment, fundraising, mobilization and organization (Smith 2000; Ward and Gibson 1998). Parties also use digital technology to engage in sophisticated information-gathering practices that enable them to craft highly customized campaign appeals. Here, parties combine electronic voters lists made available by state electoral authorities with information they gather themselves, survey and polling information they commission, publicly available databases as well as databases purchased from commercial data-gathering firms, and integrate and process these to yield sophisticated demographic and opinion information. Using this information, parties are able to fine-tune and customize their campaign appeals, often crafting detailed profiles of constituencies, electoral districts, neighbourhoods, and even individual households and voters (Carty et al. 2000: 200–10). Finally, it is also the case that, to a significantly greater extent than do government or parliamentary websites, political party sites enable various forms of interactivity. These include links to e-mail addresses of party officials and elected representatives or candidates, online feedback forms and discussion forums, online public opinion polls and, in some cases, opportunities to vote for leadership candidates or contribute to policy discussions. However, critics contend that these interactive functions are still underdeveloped relative to propaganda functions, and that it remains unclear to what extent they are actually connected to real prospects of affecting party policy outcomes (Gibson and Ward 1998; Margolis and Resnick 2000; Nixon and Johansson 1999). In this respect, it is far from clear that the use of new information and communication technologies by established mainstream political parties represents a qualitative improvement in the practices of electoral and representative democracy that have, of late, been the source of such widespread disaffection in Western liberal democracies.

Even if governments and political parties chose to capitalize creatively on the interactive capacities of digital communication technology to provide for robust, democratic engagement, it is not at all clear that a majority, or even a significant minority, of citizens would take advantage of this opportunity. Earlier in this chapter, evidence was presented that suggests very few people in the supposedly 'advanced' democracies of the capitalist West have much interest in using new information and communication technologies for explicitly political purposes, let alone to engage, on a regular basis, in demanding forms of deliberative participation. As Castells astutely observes, 'In a world of widespread crisis of political legitimacy, and citizens' disaffection vis-à-vis their representatives, the interactive, multi-directional channel of communication provided by the Internet finds few active takers *on both sides of the link*' (Castells 2001: 156; emphasis added). The reasons for this dynamic of chronic depoliticization are no doubt complex, and it is not my suggestion here that the internet is uniquely, or even primarily, to blame for it. Nevertheless, the proposition that the internet might somehow overcome this dynamic is equally dubious. Even Castells, who generally sees the internet as a transformative technology, opts for moderation in his assessment of the likelihood of the medium serving to radically democratize conventional politics: 'In fact, it would be surprising if the Internet reverses, by means of its technology, what is a deep-seated political distrust among the majority of citizens throughout the world . . . The Internet cannot provide a technological fix to the crisis of democracy' (Castells 2001: 156).

What about the possibility that the internet might provide a medium for a more vigorous and inclusive public sphere of democratic political dialogue and debate independent of government and the party system? It has been suggested that the internet holds out promise to act as a radically democratized public sphere, capable even of overcoming the biases and exclusions that undermine existing liberal democratic politics (Poster 2001: 171–88). There are many reasons to be sceptical of this view. For example, it has been suggested that the most likely impact of network communication on the public sphere is that it will contribute to a condition of 'accelerated pluralism' (Bimber 1998). This means an acceleration of the existing tendencies of liberal democratic politics as a contest between groups of people mobilized around narrowly defined interests, but who are little interested in politics beyond their own particular issue. Such pluralism has long been a characteristic of most liberal democracies, and it is not entirely unhealthy from a democratic perspective. But critics worry that the internet will exaggerate the negative aspects of pluralism, whereby the public sphere fragments into many small groups pursuing their private interests against, or in isolation from, others, without really engaging each with others concerning the common good (Sunstein 2001). Todd Gitlin has labelled this as a transformation from a comprehensive, common public sphere to a constellation of independent and proliferating 'public sphericules', and sees it as a democratic liability rather than a benefit (Gitlin 1998).

Additionally, while it is true that the internet can be inclusive in ways that other media are not, it is far from clear that participation in this medium meets the standards of equality necessary to declare it an adequately democratic public sphere. Serious material inequalities characterize access to, and use of digital technologies. In the first place, levels of access to new information and communication technologies mirror existing unequal distributions of power and resources in society, with access to the internet coinciding with existing indexes of social-economic inequality and disadvantage (Norris 2001: 68–94). Secondly, it is also the case that even those who do have 'access' to these technologies are far from equal. While everyone has the potential to be an independent producer, distributor and gatherer of information via the internet, the fact remains that most people, most of the time, experience this medium much as they do any other mass communication medium: as an audience that is relatively powerless in relation to those who control the design, content and deployment of the medium. Finally, we return again to the unfortunate reality that most users simply do not employ digital technologies in order to engage in the kinds of political activities characteristic of a democratic public sphere. Most people, most of the time, experience digital technologies as technologies of work, consumption, entertainment and socializing. In this respect, it is possible to argue that these technologies have been at least as instrumental to a radical privatization of the public sphere as they have been to its radical democratization (Barney 2003). As Lincoln Dahlberg observes, before the internet can make a meaningful contribution to a more democratic public sphere, democratic societies will have to confront the fact of 'citizens who have been socialized within a commercialized and individualized culture hostile towards public deliberation', and devise a way of generating in them a compelling sense of why they should engage in political life at all (Dahlberg 2001: 615). This is a cultural, not a technical matter. Thus, as Dahlberg concludes, 'the public sphere will not be extended merely through the diffusion of a new technological artefact' (Dahlberg 2001: 630).

This chapter began with the observation that information and communication technologies are central to the organization and exercise of political power and agency. Nothing in the ensuing discussion should detract from an appreciation of the ways in which digital networks confirm this basic fact. Digital information and communication technologies have certainly been instrumental to political practices characteristic of the network society. What remains subject to debate is the exact contours and combination of transformation and continuity that characterize these politics. We have discussed the relationship between networks and the dynamics of decline and crisis that are said to have beset the sovereign nation-state in the era of globalization. We have discussed the arguments surrounding the suggestion that we are in the midst of a 'new politics' characterized by cultural struggle, informational politics and new social movements that have taken considerable advantage of the possibilities extended by network technologies. And we have discussed the outcomes of the encounter between these technologies and the traditional institutions of liberal democratic politics. Even after these discussions, one is hard pressed to set out the essential attributes of the politics of the network society. One thing that has emerged quite consistently, however, is that the network society appears to pose challenges to the institutionalization of participatory, egalitarian, inclusive, public-spirited, democratic politics that are at least as formidable as the opportunities it presents for the same.

5
Network Identity

To this point, we have considered the network society thesis in terms of technology, economy and politics. This survey leaves an important question outstanding: *what about me?* The 'me' in the preceding sentence refers not to me, the author of this book, but rather to the category of 'me', which is to say it refers to the question of human *identity*. Identity is a complex notion. The word derives from the Latin *idem* for 'the same'. Its primary meaning refers to the quality of sameness. This suggests that identity takes on meaning only in relationships: when two things are the same as each other, we say they exhibit an identity, they are *identical*. Identity is also implicated in the human practices of naming and classification. When we name something we *identify* it, and through this *identification* we fix what that thing is, by classifying it with other things that it is like, and apart from other things that it is unlike. Thus, identity is established in and by relationships both of similarity and difference, association and distinction, collectivity and singularity.

In relation to human beings, identity is the word we use to denote our consciousness of who we are, our sense of our most significant or defining attributes. In short – and the association between these words is no accident – my *identity* is comprised of the *ideas* that others have about me, and the ideas I have about my 'self'. As with all things, the identity of a human person is established in and by the relationships of similarity and difference she enjoys with other things – including, especially, other persons. Human identity reflects both a person's associations with, and her distinction from, other persons. Beyond this basic conception, however, there exists considerable debate about the nature and operation of human identity. Where does a person's identity come from? Can a person choose her identity, or is it something assigned to her by others? Does it derive from characteristics internal to a person, or from the environment in which she exists? Is the source of identity primarily spiritual, intellectual, cultural or biological? Is identity a reflection of natural attributes, or is it socially constructed? What are the most important contributors to a person's identity? Is identity constant and immutable, or is it historically contingent and dynamic?

This list of questions could be much longer, and this is not the place to attempt to solve the difficult controversies that surround the notion of identity in the contemporary context. It will suffice here to state the obvious: identity is a crucial component of human subjectivity, of the experience of being a conscious actor in the world. It is, therefore, not surprising that accounts of life in the network society include claims about a reorientation of the human experience of identity in association with changes occurring in the technological, economic and political organization of human life. This chapter will investigate the question of identity as it is discussed in the discourse surrounding the network society. It will also consider two phenomena that are customarily linked closely with issues of identity – community and culture – and which also figure prominently in discussions of the network society.

Identity *versus* networks

As discussed briefly in chapter 1, in Castells's formulation, the logic of identity takes on a particular importance in the network society. The salience of identity is both accelerated by the prevailing conditions of the network society, and also a crucial source of social and political resistance to these conditions. As Castells puts it:

In a world of global flows of wealth, power and images, the search for identity, collective or individual, ascribed or constructed, becomes the fundamental source of social meaning ... Identity is becoming the main, and sometimes the only, source of meaning in a historical period characterized by widespread destructuring of organizations, delegitimization of institutions, fading away of major social movements, and ephemeral cultural expressions. People increasingly organize their meaning not around what they do, but on the basis of what they are, or believe they are ... Our societies are increasingly structured around a bipolar opposition between the net and the self. (Castells 1996: 3)

Here, identity is presented as an energetic dialectical force opposing the dislocating dynamics of the network society. Identity emerges as the alienated 'other' of globalization, of 'timeless time', and of the placelessness of the 'space of flows'. This 'other' appears both within and beyond the reach of global networks. Within this reach, identity emerges as an organizing force amongst those who experience the network society as one in which their autonomy is diminished, in which global forces threaten to reduce their particularity and distinction to homogeneity, and in which the power to define the conditions of their existence is decreasingly located in actors and institutions over which they might hope to have direct influence. Identity also thrives in those areas of the world where existence remains intensely local and membership in the cosmopolitan community is not an option, by virtue of systematic exclusion from global technological, economic and political networks. Thus, enforced cosmopolitanism as well as enforced localism – systemic by-products of the network society – each, in their own way, catalyse what Castells describes as the *power of identity*.

According to Castells, characteristic of the network society is a 'widespread surge of powerful expressions of collective identity that challenge globalization and cosmopolitanism on behalf of cultural singularity and people's control over their lives and environment' (Castells 1997: 2). The political mobilization of identity is certainly not new. What is remarkable about the network society is the extent to which identity persists as a social and political force despite the supposedly universalizing spirit of global networks, technologies and markets. A second distinctive mark of the network society is that, departing from the historical norm of the modern period, the nation-state is no longer the only, and probably not even the most significant, mobilizer or carrier of political identity. According to Castells, the primacy and power of identity in (and against) the network society is embodied and carried by a variety of social movements, some of which are organized nationally but many of which are not, and whose bases of identification (i.e., of constructing meaning) are many and varied.

In *The Power of Identity* (1997: 8–10), Castells distils a diverse literature to set out three distinct categories of identity. *Legitimizing identities* are those induced by a society's dominant institutions and ideology, in order to reflect, support and rationalize its structure of social roles and relationships, including relationships of power and authority, inclusion and exclusion, and domination and subordination. These identities establish the boundaries of civil society in a given context. An example of legitimizing identity is national citizenship, defined according to the laws and institutions of the nation-state, which constructs the boundaries of a country's civil society, and establishes relationships of inclusion and exclusion relative to the rights, obligations, benefits and protections of citizenship. *Resistance identities* are formed on the basis of opposition to, exclusion from, or subordination under, the legitimizing identities of a given society and its institutions. Exclusion, marginalization and subordination in relation to the dominant categories of society give rise to defensive communal identities that challenge the legitimacy of the prevailing order and institutions of civil society. These resistance identities typically congeal around the very bases of their exclusion or marginalization from mainstream civil society – their biology (race, sex); their history (class, ethnic or religious minorities); their geography (regional minorities). Thus, for example, liberal feminist identity congeals around the exclusion, domination and subordination of women in mainstream civil society based on sex, and drives the case for 'women's rights'. In such cases, resistance identities act to 'revers[e] the value judgment while reinforcing the boundary' (Castells 1997: 9). Identities of this sort challenge the structure of civil society to become less suppressive of difference, more accommodating and inclusive. Besides feminist identity, examples under this category include the African-American identity associated with the civil rights movement in the United States, and a variety of identities that have formed around subordinated, regionally concentrated, ethnic and religious minorities throughout the world.

Finally, *project identities* arise when 'social actors, on the basis of whichever cultural materials are available to them, build a new identity that redefines their position in society and, by so doing, seek the transformation of the overall social structure' (Castells 1997: 8). These identities also resist and challenge the legitimacy of civil society as it is constructed by the dominant categories and institutions. However, they differ from resistance identities in two respects. First, they do not congeal around categories that simply reflect the bases of exclusion/subordination coded into the legitimizing identities of a given society – they establish entirely new identity categories. Second, unlike resistance identities, project identities do not aim at inclusion or acceptance in mainstream civil society as it is constructed – they seek transformation of that society. An example of this sort of identity is that formed around the global environmental movement, or perhaps even the identities that drive and are sustained by the international peace movement.

In Castells's view, the rise of network society is marked by a collapse of the legitimacy of legitimizing identities, as a result of economic globalization, technological dynamism and the declining inclination and ability of nation-states and other traditional institutions (including, especially, the patriarchal family) to impart to their adherents a sense of autonomy and efficacy, or to deliver the social welfare necessary to secure their ongoing allegiance and consent. This crisis of legitimizing identities results in, and to a certain extent *from*, the proliferation of a great variety of resistance identities, to which individuals increasingly turn in an effort to localize meaning and to establish autonomy, against the dislocated powerlessness and meaninglessness they experience in the shadow of economic and technological globalization, and in the eclipse of the traditions of modern industrial society. As

Castells describes them, these resistance identities are 'defensive reactions' against the threats to traditional social organization posed by globalization, the logic of networking and flexibility, and the (alleged) collapse of patriarchal family relations (Castells 1997: 65–6). It is in this respect that 'the self', or identity, emerges as a comprehensive, though diversified, counterforce to 'the net', or the global network society.

These threats motivate social movements built around resistance identities in a variety of forms. These include *religious fundamentalisms*, such as those witnessed in the rise of both Islamic fundamentalism and American Christian fundamentalism; ethnic and minority *nationalisms*, such as those that accelerated in the wake of the dissolution of the Soviet Union, as well as other examples including Kurdish, Catalunyan and Quebecois nationalisms; and *territorial communes* that cohere around the location of identity at the urban level, whether in progressive urban reform movements or reactionary, gated residential enclaves that seek to purify community within the gates and to shut out the complexity of the world outside (Castells 1997: 12–64). Movements such as these, as well as those deriving from other bases of resistance, signify, according to Castells, the power of identity thrust in the face of the network society.

What about project identity? Project identity emerges from the radicalization of resistance identity, when a group of people who are marginalized or subordinated in civil society do not simply seek inclusion (on the very terms of their exclusion), but rather reject the society that rejects them, and seek to transform it. Such project identities are highly and self-consciously politicized, and they represent a diversity of ideological positions. So, for example, Castells highlights 'three movements that explicitly oppose[d] the new global order of the 1990s' (Castells 1997: 69): the Zapatista rebels in Chiapas, Mexico; the right-wing American militia and Patriot movement; and Japan's Aum Shinrikyo cult – each of which was driven by a commitment to significantly alternative ways of organizing social life in their respective locations. Less extremist, but still radical, project identities have also formed around deep concern for the fate of the global ecological system, and round the fundamental challenge to patriarchal society represented by the international women's movement (Castells 1997: 110–242). We might also include here the nascent anti-globalization movement that emerged at the end of the 1990s, though it still remains unclear whether the constituents of this loose and dynamic coalition in fact identify with a coherent, positive, common project beyond their shared opposition to various manifestations of transnational capitalism and American hegemony. In any case, in Castells's estimation, hope for social change in the information age lies in the conversion of progressive resistance identities into projects aimed at fundamental transformation (Castells 1997: 12).

In chapter 4, we considered the intimate connection between new social movements and new information and communication technologies characteristic of the politics of the network society. Consideration of movements based on resistance and project identities suggests that, in many cases, this relationship is an ambivalent one. On one hand, movements driven by identities developed in opposition to the 'new global order' are, in effect, opposed to the order built by network technology. Across the range of their ideological diversity, social movements based on oppositional identities are driven, at least in part, by 'the abstraction of power in a web of computers [that is] disintegrating existing mechanisms of social control and political representation', and they are linked in 'refusing globalization for the sake of capital and informationalization for the sake of technology' (Castells 1997: 69, 71). On the other hand, as described in the preceding chapter, the relationship between new social movements and new information and communication technologies could be described as umbilical. Computer networks provide the lifeline that nourishes these social formations. In Castells's formulation, 'The powerful impact of each of these movements has come, to a large extent, from their media presence and from their effective use of information technology . . . New communication technologies are fundamental for these movements to exist' (Castells 1997: 106–7). In the network society, 'the net' and 'the self' may be opposed, but they are also inextricably joined.

Identity as network

Not everyone who experiences the centrifugal energies of globalization and network technology develops resistance or project identities that implicate them in social movements seeking to contest the prevailing order of civil society. This, however, is not to say that their identities, and identity-forming practices, remain unaffected by the dynamics of globalization and the new technologies. Indeed, even for those who do not identify themselves *against* the prevailing currents of contemporary society, the present condition can be understood as one in which questions of identity are present for individuals, on a personal level, in a very immediate way. It is to this that Anthony Giddens refers when he describes the late modern condition as a 'post-traditional order' in which 'the self becomes a reflexive project' (Giddens 1991: 32). Inhabitants of the late modern West have witnessed a gradual eclipse of many of their traditional sources of meaning and identification, including organized religious and other moral codes; homogeneous national cultures; stable, extended and intergenerational family ties; predictable, long-term careers; and even extended domicile in the same geographic location. The salience of these and other traditional sources of meaning and identity have waned for many people in contemporary, late capitalist societies, leaving subjects with the task of reflexively building, rather than passively accepting, their identities. Once, questions about 'who we are' were the more or less exclusive province of poets, philosophers and priests. Now, late modern individuals live out the question 'who am I?' in their daily 'lifestyle choices'. As Giddens puts it: 'The more tradition loses its hold, and the more daily life is reconstituted in terms of the dialectical interplay of the local and the global, the more individuals are forced to negotiate lifestyle choices among a diversity of options . . . Reflexively organized life planning . . . becomes a central feature of the structuring of self-identity' (Giddens 1991: 1, 5). As discussed in chapter 1, postmodern thinkers have extended this conception of identity even further, suggesting that almost nothing of identity is simply 'received'. Instead, identity is something practised *upon* people in the processes through which they are inserted into social relationships, and something practised *by* people in the appropriations they accomplish in the generation and circulation of social discourse. Postmodern identity is constructed as a complex pastiche of relationships, choices and acts, enacted in a variety of parallel and overlapping contexts. Rather than being a fixed, natural and unchanging condition corresponding to a stable situation and set of attributes, postmodern identity is artificial, fluid, contingent, multifaceted and mutable.

It is, one might say, a lot like a network. And so it is not surprising that the proliferation of personal access to network technology and the elaboration of the postmodern identity condition are often presented as enjoying a certain affinity. Perhaps the most prominent account of this affinity is given by Sherry Turkle, whose book *Life on the Screen* (1995) explores the social domain of multi-user online environments, and captures perfectly the purported symmetry between digital networks and postmodern identity. According to Turkle, 'computers are not just changing our lives, but changing our selves' (Turkle 2001: 236). Computers, in this line of thinking, *change* our selves by providing us with a novel instrument for the self-directed social *construction* of our selves. Online, writes Turkle, 'the self is constructed and the rules of social interaction are built, not received' (Turkle 1995: 10). Being online means 'inventing ourselves as we go along . . . you are who you pretend to be . . . your identity on the computer is the sum of your distributed presence . . . an identity so fluid and so multiple it strains the limits of the notion' (Turkle 1995: 10–12). Indeed, as opposed to being singular, authentic and fixed, identity online is described by Turkle as multiple, simulated, and infinitely revisable. Network-mediated practices of the self 'imply difference, multiplicity, heterogeneity and fragmentation . . . Traditional ideas about identity have been tied to a notion of authenticity that such virtual experiences actively subvert . . . the self is not only decentred, but multiplied without limit' (Turkle 2001: 242). In relation to people whose daily experiences are immersed in the technologies of the network society, the question that defines identity is not so much 'Who am I?' but, rather, 'Who am we?' (Turkle 2001: 236).

Several of the technical affordances of the network media environment lend themselves to the postmodern identity condition described by Turkle. The first is the dislocated, deterritorialized character of network communications, which can diminish geographic location as a decisive factor in the determination of identity, at least for those cosmopolitans to whom connectivity affords a means of virtual escape from locality. In the online environment, where a person is '@', where she can 'go' and what she can 'get' are more significant, in terms of identity, than where she is, or where she is from. Secondly, network communication is disembodied, and does not require physical co-presence for routine interpersonal interaction. The human body has traditionally represented a relatively fixed, stable basis of identification, and a medium that enables communication without bodies co-present in time and space diminishes the impact of the body as a marker of identity in social interaction. Disembodiment takes on added significance in conjunction with the opacity of digital communication. Networks are, for the most part, opaque media that cannot be seen through. This opacity effectively eliminates the impact of visual apprehension of physical appearance and behaviour which, for better or for worse, have traditionally been strongly tied to identity. Identity markers like sex, skin colour, body shape, age and dress are apparent through online interaction only when information signalling them is volunteered, and even then it cannot be relied upon.

Together, the dislocation, disembodiment and opacity of network communication can enable a high degree of anonymity and fluidity in the social construction of our selves, and materialize the postmodern account of identity. Online, the potential is there for people to construct identities as they choose, rather than having their 'self' determined for them based on prejudicial attributes like location, body or physical attributes. As Cameron Bailey observes, 'It would seem clear that the safety of binary oppositions – self/other, black/white, male/female, straight/gay, writer/reader – would evaporate in the forcefully uncertain world of electronic discourse. A message comes and goes without a face, communication takes place without bodies to ground it ... In the online world, identity is often chosen, played with, subverted or foregrounded as a construct . . . none of the usual land-marks can be trusted . . .' (Bailey 2001: 335). And, on the network, people can choose more than one identity, and revise these multiple identities with relative ease, ensuring that their 'self' is no more held hostage to their history than it is to their name, body or whereabouts. In this configur-ation, self, or identity, is not just *mediated* by network tech-nology. It also, *in itself*, takes on the attributes of a network – a lattice of nodes linked by ties of varying strength and duration, through which identity is practised, rather than simply borne, as the ebb and flow of information.

Many commentators present this situation as progressive, insofar as digital networks have served as an instrument and arena of liberation from the prejudice, oppression and injus-tice characteristic of pre-modern and modern constellations of identity. In the network society, rather than simply receiv-ing an identity that 'naturalizes' or 'essentializes' arbitrary classifications of ethno-racial origin, geographic location and sexed bodies, people are technologically enabled to control the conditions of their own representation/identity. Cyber-space has thus been presented as particularly liberating for people historically assigned identities that they experience primarily as the basis for their exclusion, marginalization, domination and subordination. Arguments have been made, and evidence presented, for the emancipatory potential of the network environment for women (Haraway 1991; Hayles 1999; Plant 1997; Stone 1992), racial minorities (Kolko et al. 2000) and gays and lesbians (Morton 1999; Wakeford 1997; Woodland 1995). In the network environment, dislocation, disembodiment and opaque communication mean that women, non-whites, and non-heterosexuals can perform their identities as they wish, rather than simply being assigned a construction of their 'natural' identity that serves interests other than their own, and which they might not be happy to simply accept. It has been suggested that the contributions network media make to the viability of liberated identity and subject positions hold out the possibility of a more inclu-sive and pluralistic democratic public sphere (Poster 2001: 183–8).

This assessment of the progressive prospects of identity building in the age of network technology is not universally shared. Some have argued that, whatever its progressive potential, the disembodiment and anonymity enabled by network mediated interaction simply evade the very real problems of discrimination and injustice based on identity in the material, offline world, rather than addressing their substance. Here, the convergence of postmodernism and cyberspace produces a realm of hyper-aesthetic, depoliticized solipsism, in which 'the reality of the real world is disavowed, the coherence of the self deconstructed into fragments, and the quality of experience reduced to sensation and intoxication . . . [and] empowerment entails a refusal to recognize the substantive and independent reality of others, and to be involved in relations of mutual dependency and responsibility' (Robins 2000: 84–5). This leads to questions about the ethical implications of the intersection between network technologies and the postmodern identity condition. Remarking on 'the promotion of an anonymity which enables flexible, multiple and anonymous identity construction', Michelle Willson worries that 'the dissolution or fragmentation of the subject and the instantaneous, transient nature of all communication disconnect or abstract the individual from physical action and a sense of social and personal responsibility to others' (Willson 2000: 650). Others have suggested that disembodiment robs communication of the risk conditions that give it substance and meaning and encourage moderation of the nihilistic assertion of personal will without regard for limits (Dreyfus 2001).

These normative criticisms of simulated, networked identity bear consideration, but the points they make might be moot, as might the general claim that network media such as the internet constitute a significant site for postmodern practices of identity construction. It is possible that characterizations of the internet as a medium of extensive postmodern identity fabrication are exaggerated, insofar as they over-generalize anecdotal evidence of practices that are actually quite marginal in relation to the tendencies of mainstream internet use. Recent empirical evidence suggests that very few people use the internet to engage regularly in practices of alternative identity construction. As Castells points out in reference to this evidence, 'Role-playing and identity-building as the basis of on-line interaction are a tiny proportion of Internet based sociability, and this kind of practice seems to be heavily concentrated among teenagers . . . role playing is a telling social experience, but one that does not represent a significant proportion of social interaction on the Internet nowadays' (Castells 2001: 118–19). Perhaps these teenagers will continue to adopt multiple alternative personae as they mature into adult users of the medium, but it is equally plausible that they will not. Those who do seek to perform identities that are alternative to those they are assigned in the material world will probably continue to find a hospitable stage for this performance on the internet. However, one might also expect that most people, most of the time will approach the medium simply *bearing* an identity, rather than with the intention of consciously making a new, or another, one. Similarly, it is possible that emphasis on anonymity in online interaction obscures a crucial point regarding identity in the context of internet-mediated communication. As theorists and analysts of surveillance and privacy remind us, the digital environment is one in which anonymity is something that is nearly impossible to achieve – to operate in the network society is to be exhaustively identified, constantly monitored and incessantly categorized (Lyon 2001; Whitaker 1999). In this light, it could be argued that digital technologies have instantiated a condition in which people are *less* in control of their identities than ever before.

Network community

Closely linked to the question of identity in the network society is the question of community. Discussion of the relationship between networks and community has proliferated in recent years, but it is complicated by the highly contested nature of the meaning of the word 'community'. In contemporary discourse, 'community' can signal many things. It can refer to a geographic location, a place where people live or, perhaps more accurately, a congregation of people who live in a common place, such as a neighbourhood, a town or a city. It can refer to a group of people who share a common identity, common traits, a common set of values or a common way of life, such as a religious community, an ethnic community, or the 'gay community'. A community can be a group of people who associate based on a set of mutual, common or shared interests, such as the 'business community', the 'environmental community' or various 'fan communities'. Additionally, the definitive practices of community can vary considerably. For example, community can denote associations in which very little communication takes place, and also associations in which *nothing but* communication takes place. Finally, there is little agreement on the character of relationship necessary for an association to merit the label 'community'. For some, community requires 'thick' relationships of mutual moral obligation, bound by strong, enduring multiplex ties and practices that define social roles, norms and identity, and are not easily broken. For others, 'community' can feature relatively 'thin' relationships comprised of voluntary, revocable, dynamic ties based on shared individual interests and needs.

The question of the relationship between network technology and community is made problematic by this complexity. Still, it cannot be ignored. Identity and community are organically related, and communication technologies have long been identified as central to the constitution, maintenance and character of communities. In the 1950s, Harold Innis argued that the balance between time-bias and space-bias in a society's prevailing means of communication (i.e., whether communication is oriented towards locality and endurance in time, or reach and speed across space) is decisive in terms of the possibility and structure of community in that society (Innis 1951). Decades later, James Carey distinguished between the 'transmission' and 'ritual' functions of communication, the latter understood as an ongoing cultural practice of sharing information within groups that is constitutive of community, especially in its 'thick' variants (Carey 1989). And many thinkers have pointed to the significance of technologically mediated communication in the construction and maintenance of large-scale communities, in which lack of physical proximity means that communal bonds are formed not so much between people who interact routinely and directly, but rather between people who identify with a common symbolic order, the elements of which are transmitted to them in common via mass communication technologies.

This raises an interesting issue that, as we will see, has been significant in the debates around network technology and community. The idea that mediated communication could somehow substitute for geographic proximity as a basis of community has been around for a long time. Writing in 1916, John Dewey observed that 'Persons do not become a society by living in physical proximity, any more than a man ceases to be socially influenced by being so many feet or miles removed from others. A book or a letter may institute a more intimate association between human beings separated thousands of miles from each other than exists between dwellers under the same roof' (Dewey 1964: 4–5). Forty years ago Melvin Webber raised the possibility that modern urbanization, characteristically associated with decline in organic communal relationships, provided for 'community without propinquity' (Webber 1963). In the age of mass communication and transportation technologies, communities need not be geographically localized, he argued, nor do they require immediate, face-to-face encounters. More recently, Benedict Anderson, reflecting on the role of the printing press in establishing communal identification on the scale of the nation-state, writes, 'all communities larger than primordial villages of face-to-face contact are imagined . . . imagined because the members of even the smallest nation will never know most of their fellow members, meet them, or even hear of them, yet in the minds of each lives the image of their communion' (Anderson 1983). As people less and less occupy a localized, common physical space, communication technologies, in a sense, become the space of community.

On the other hand, it has been argued that the proliferation of communication technologies is implicated in what is best understood as a long-term decline in the vitality of community in the modern West. This sense of the decline of community under modern conditions was expressed as early as the late nineteenth century by Ferdinand Tönnies (1964), who saw in the rise of the industrial, capitalist, liberal state a shift from traditional, obligatory, personalized communal relationships (*gemeinschaft* or 'community') to more legal, voluntary, impersonal social relationships (*gesellschaft* or 'society'). The perception that 'community' is failing under modern conditions has escalated in the latter decades of the twentieth century. In a book called *Habits of the Heart* (1985), Robert Bellah and his colleagues argue that the institutionalization of the ideologies of liberal individualism and capitalist consumerism in the 1980s and 1990s have undermined the possibility of community – by overvaluing individual achievement, competition and self-realization and undervaluing the common good, cooperation and civic identity. Robert Putnam (2000) makes a similar argument, and documents a decline in membership in voluntary civic associations in the United States over the past few decades as a signal of a dangerous decline in 'social capital' – the energy and resources available for common projects and enterprises in the common interest. Interestingly, many of those who have diagnosed a decline of community identify in their diagnoses the very instruments that are supposed to make 'imaginary' communities possible under modern conditions: communication technologies. It could be, and has been, argued that communication technologies do not so much overcome the spatial separateness and lack of proximity of contemporary social life as they *support* and even *encourage* it. Communication technologies, notably television, have been identified by some as having a delocalizing, atomizing, privatizing effect that, far from making meaningful community possible, fatally weakens it. In this view, these technologically mediated communities are not communities at all. They are, rather, at best 'pseudocommunities' which have the appearance, but not the substance, of genuine communities (Beniger 1987).

It is in the context of these debates that we can locate the question of community and network technology. It is clear that digital networks provide a venue for sociability and communicative interaction. As Steve Jones characterizes it, 'Computer-mediated communication, of course, is not just a tool, it is at once technology, medium and engine of social relations. It not only structures social relations, it is the space within which the relations occur and the tool that individuals use to enter that space' (Jones 1999: 224). The question is whether the technological space digital networks provide for sociability is likely to be conducive to strengthened community, or just another contribution to its continued weakness.

For some, the advent and spread of network technology brings with it the promise of a rejuvenation of community engagement and solidarity, a promise denied by preceding technologies of mass communication, such as print and television, which lacked the capacity for multiplex, interactive communication provided by the internet. There is a considerable discourse that insists not only that the internet will succeed where previous mass communication technologies have failed, but also that it will reverse their pathological effects vis-à-vis community. As Jones observes,

> Critical to the rhetoric surrounding the information highway is the promise of a renewed sense of community and, in many instances, new types and formations of community. Computer-mediated communication, it seems, will do by way of electronic pathways what cement roads were unable to do, namely, connect us rather than atomize us, put us at the controls of a vehicle and yet not detach us from the rest of the world. (Jones 1999: 220)

Much of the early attention to whether this promise would be realized was devoted to the question of 'virtual community'. So-called virtual communities exist entirely online: they are extra-geographical, non-localized aggregations of individuals whose interaction is carried out exclusively across computer networks, via their participation in electronic mailing-lists, multiple-user domains, weblogs, chat and bulletin-board services and discussion groups. Among the earliest, and most influential, attempts to articulate this idea and give an account of its manifestation in practice was Howard Rheingold's *The Virtual Community* (1993), in which he recounts his experience as a pioneer of the legendary Whole Earth 'Lectronic Link (WELL) – a global, computer-mediated network of multiple discussion groups. There are many possible variants of virtual community. What they all seem to have in common (besides mediation by digital networks) is that communication is their core and definitive activity, that membership in them is voluntary and easily revocable, and that the basis of relationship is primarily shared personal interest, rather than some form of obligation.

Predictably, assessments of the virtual community phenomenon have been mixed. Supporters argue that virtual communities overcome the obstacles of scale, including time, distance and population size, that make community so difficult to practise under the geographic and demographic conditions of modern nation-states and cities (Coate 1997). Virtual communities – because they are mediated by devices that are accessible in the private sphere of the home, and because networks enable 24-hour asynchronous communication – are also often presented as more convenient than other forms of community engagement. It is also often suggested that virtual communities are more meaningful than other forms of community because they are volitional (i.e., people seek them out), rather than based on the arbitrary or 'accidental' foundations of geographic proximity, common ethnicity or shared ancestry (Bruckman 1998; Wellman and Gulia 1999). The online environment of virtual communities is portrayed as providing a healthy, secure and accessible alternative to the erosion, insecurity and inaccessibility of public spaces for community interaction in the physical, offline world (Fernback 1999). Virtual communities are also presented as less hierarchical and less discriminatory, more egalitarian and inclusive than traditional communities, where recourse to visual markers of identity often results in prejudicial exclusion, silencing and mistreatment. In a related argument, it is suggested that virtual communities make it possible for individuals to represent or 'identify' themselves as they choose in a multiplicity of community interactions, including the adoption of multiple or changing personae, as they desire (Turkle 1995). Finally, the nature of technological mediation in virtual communities makes it far easier to enter and exit at will than is possible in offline communities. This ease of entry and exit, combined with voluntarism and a basis in freely expressed interests, allows virtual communities to emerge as the perfect solution to the 'problem' of community in the contemporary context, by maximizing autonomy and choice without wholly sacrificing the possibility of communal attachment, and vice versa (Wilbur 1997).

On the other side of the ledger, critics have been quick to point out the possible shortcomings of virtual community. In the first place, it is argued that the dislocation and disem-

bodiment of network communication undermine the rootedness in place and body that is necessary for a robust experience of, and commitment to, community (Willson 2000).
Others are concerned that the ease and convenience of online
interaction will further encourage withdrawal from civic
engagement offline, and a deepening privatization of social
life (Lockard 1997; Doheny-Farina 1996). Related criticisms
emerge from the ability of online inhabitants to customize
their social encounters and spaces to suit their narrow interests. The proliferation of personalized communities of interest runs the risk of fragmenting general interest communities
to the point of dissolution, and insulating the members of
these relatively parochial communities of interest from
ongoing encounters with the difference, diversity and heterogeneity that populate the offline world (Sunstein 2001). It
has also been suggested that the combination of voluntary
attachments based on personal interests and ease of entry and
exit undermines the sort of binding social and moral obligations that convert relationships from market contracts into
communities (Galston 1999). Finally, critics suggest that the
anonymity characteristic of interaction in virtual communities erodes the foundation of responsibility, accountability
and social trust upon which meaningful communities are
built (Bimber 1998). Bruce Bimber captures the spirit of this
range of criticisms well when he writes: 'our understanding
of the content of social interaction on the Net gives little
reason to think that community will be significantly enhanced
on a large scale. Building community in a normatively rich
sense is not the same as increasing the amount of social talk,
and there is good reason to think the latter will be the norm
on the Net' (Bimber 1998: 148). Bimber concludes that the
most likely effect of network communication on community
is that it will contribute to an 'accelerated pluralism', in
which 'thin' communities (associations of individuals whose
private interests are complementary) will proliferate but
'thick' community (wherein members collectively pursue
goals beyond the sum of their mutual private interests) is
unlikely to be enhanced.

These controversies are not easily solved, but evidence has
begun to emerge that suggests they are perhaps tangential
to the broader question of how network technology affects

community practice and engagement. As with the practices of alternative and multiple identity-construction discussed above, it would seem that relatively few users of network technology participate regularly or frequently in purely virtual communities, and that routine engagement with exclusively online communities represents a very small proportion of overall internet use (Howard et al. 2002: 56). In his recent work, Castells synthesizes these findings as follows: 'the uses of the Internet are, overwhelmingly, instrumental, and closely connected to the work, family and everyday life of Internet users . . . While chat rooms, news groups and multi-purpose Internet conferences were meaningful for early Internet users, their quantitative and qualitative importance has dwindled with the spread of the Internet' (Castells 2001: 118). This suggests that if we are interested in the relationship between network technology and the prospects of community, perhaps 'virtual' community is not the place to look.

Accordingly, social scientists have turned away from speculative questions about virtual community, and towards empirical study of the internet in 'everyday life'. Here, researchers investigate how individuals integrate network technologies into their repertoires of communicative and social activity more generally, and many have concentrated specifically on the question of whether and how internet use affects patterns of social and community engagement, both online and offline. Some early studies found evidence of a correlation between increased internet use and social withdrawal, and an association between internet use and declining communication with family and friends, a decline in the size of users' social circles, and increased depression and loneliness (Kraut et al. 1998; National Public Radio et al. 2000; Nie and Erbring 2000). Confirming their earlier findings, Norman Nie and his colleagues have recently argued that, 'On average, the more time spent on the Internet, the less time spent with friends, family, and colleagues. Alternatively, the more time spent on the Internet, the more time spent alone' (Nie et al. 2002: 238–9).

However, a considerable body of evidence has emerged to contradict these findings. A study based on data derived from a comprehensive survey of visitors to the National Geographic website in 1998 concluded that 'the Internet is increasing social capital, civic engagement and developing a sense of belonging to online community' (Quan Haase et al. 2002: 319). Using data from extensive surveys in 2000, a study by the Pew Internet and American Life Project finds that e-mail use correlates positively with more intensive contact with family and friends, and more extensive social contacts more generally. Its authors conclude that 'online tools are more likely to extend social contact, rather than detract from it . . . Internet use is positively associated with social activity' (Howard et al. 2002: 68). Interestingly, this study found no correlation between internet use and a person's *overall* sense of community, suggesting that both the utopian projections of internet dreamers and the doomsday scenarios of the medium's detractors are overstated. This interpretation is more or less confirmed in a major study of internet use in Britain, in which little evidence is found that the internet independently affects individual time-use in communication activities (Anderson and Tracey 2002). A major longitudinal study in the United States comparing internet users to non-users found that internet usage 'is associated with increased community and political involvement and is associated with significant and increased online and offline social interactions' (Katz and Rice 2002: 135). Finally, in their studies of Netville – a 'wired' suburb outside Toronto – Keith Hampton and Barry Wellman found that residents with network access were more successful than those without access in maintaining mid-range and distant social ties and support networks, and also were better 'neighbours', insofar as they knew more of their fellow residents, interacted with them more frequently and were more involved in community activities. These findings lead Hampton and Wellman to conclude as follows: 'Contrary to dystopian predictions, new communication technologies do not disconnect people from communities. Computer-mediated communication reinforces existing communities, establishing contact and encouraging support where none existed before' (Hampton and Wellman 2002: 368).

These are formidable findings, but it would still be premature to conclude that we have no reason to be concerned about the fate of community in the network society. For example, most of the studies cited above focus solely on the instrumental aspects of internet use – i.e., on how people intentionally *use* the internet in their communicative social practices. It may be the case that the impact of these technologies on community might not be felt primarily in instrumental terms; perhaps what is more important is the extent to which digital networks *in their whole range of applications* affect and structure the material environment in which community practices are situated (Barney 2004). In any case, what does emerge clearly from these studies is that the internet is a perfect instrument for a world in which community is understood as a network. One might even say that the particular utilities of this technology actually encourage us to think of community in this way. Over twenty years ago, Barry Wellman and Claude Fischer argued that the equation of community with localized, geographically concentrated relationships was untenable, and that communities could be more profitably described as networks of strong and weak interpersonal ties between spatially dispersed nodes (Fischer 1982; Wellman 1979). As Wellman writes in a recent update of the relation of this thesis to digital communication technologies: 'Communities are networks of interpersonal ties that provide sociability, support, information, a sense of belonging and social identity' (Wellman 2001: 227). Communities, in this view, are not places. They are, instead, personalized networks built through the choices of the self-conscious actors at their centre. Here, community is redefined as 'networked individualism', and it reflects, rather than conditions or constrains, the choices of those who enact it.

As personalized networks, communities depend heavily for their organization and operation upon the technologies that mediate the flows of resources that pass between the nodes that comprise them. As Castells has observed, the internet has emerged as the perfect 'material support for networked individualism' (Castells 2001: 129). This pertains in relation to the medium's support of the weak, ephemeral ties characteristic of virtual communities, as well as in relation to the dynamic networks of spatially and temporally dislocated offline ties managed by the highly mobile individuals of the network society. As Castells describes, 'the most important role of the Internet in structuring social relationships is its contribution to the new pattern of sociability based on individualism . . . it is not that the Internet creates a pattern of networked individualism, but the development of the Internet provides an appropriate material support for the diffusion of networked individualism as the dominant form of sociability' (Castells 2001: 130–1). Phrased differently, we might say that digital technology is the perfect instrument for networked individuals to imagine themselves as communities. It is perfect because social relationships based on the network model require communication that can be maintained in the context of individual mobility, and despite spatial and temporal dislocation of nodes (i.e., other people). The defining practices and activities of life in the network society are decreasingly located in consistent, enduring proximity with others and, in societies where everything is on, open and for sale all the time, we also decreasingly share temporal rhythms with others. Digital technology contributes to this dislocation, but it also provides the means to connect or communicate with others, similarly dislocated, under these conditions.

Network culture

Like community, the word 'culture' admits of multiple, contested meanings. In its original definition as a word in the English language, *culture* referred to two related things: the art or practice of cultivation, and a medium in which things grow and can be nourished and sustained. *Cultivation* refers to the practices of preparing the conditions in which things might grow. The root of both words is the Latin *cultus*, for care. Cultivation is the practice of caring for, or tending to, things. And culture is, in this sense, the expression of that for which we care or to which we tend. This is how the word entered the English language in the fifteenth century, but its meaning has expanded and varied considerably since then. Today, we understand culture to denote the 'systems of meaning' and 'ways of life' which emerge from people's collective social practices, reflect their priorities and expectations, and subsequently condition their judgement and behaviour. Our understanding of culture has become very expansive, encompassing cultivated behaviours enacted by an identifiable group of people; any set of shared, routinized social practices, whether institutionalized or not; any set of learned ideals, values, norms, beliefs, habits and traditions; any set of symbolic or communicative representations of the foregoing. Culture consists of patterns, behaviours, symbols, and artefacts. Cultural systems may, on the one hand, be considered as products of human behaviour and symbolic action, and, on the other hand, as conditioning influences upon further behaviour and symbolic action. This last point is crucial: human beings make their cultures, and their cultures, in turn, make human beings what they are, insofar as culture provides the material and parameters for the construction and maintenance of personal and collective identity. The advent of digital network technology is widely believed to be involved in nothing less than a cultural transformation. Consider the following from the introduction to an influential collection of writing on this issue:

> To say that we inhabit a digital world is an understatement. In recent years the Internet and other information technologies have transformed many fundamental parts of life: how we work and play, how we communicate and consume, how we create knowledge and learn, even how we understand politics and participate in public life . . . The ubiquity of digital data storage, computation and telecommunication have made us profoundly dependent on computer networks (whether we realize it or not) enveloping society in what might be termed a 'digital culture'. (Trend 2001: 1)

If this is true, it is difficult to imagine where one might begin an attempt to specify the culture of the network society.

Some have looked to the cultural disposition of internet users for indications in this regard, though few have agreed on the substance of that disposition, or even what ought to be measured. For his part, Castells suggests the culture of the internet is shaped by the values of the technology's producers and initial users. In his view, the culture of the internet is one of openness, freedom and voluntary cooperation, built upon four 'layers' of definitive users: techno-elites, hackers, virtual communitarians and entrepreneurs (Castells 2001: 37). In this formulation, the techno-elite layer of internet culture of is one of 'openness . . . determined by a techno-meritocratic culture rooted in academia and science. This is a culture of belief in the inherent good of scientific and technological development as a key component of the progress of humankind' (Castells 2001: 39). The second layer of internet culture according to Castells is hacker culture – the loose affiliation of programmers who creatively and collaboratively built on the academic and scientific roots of the internet to produce the various programming languages, protocols and applications that now form the infrastructure of the internet, ranging from things like e-mail, to the web and various browsers, Linux and other open-source software packages. As Castells describes it, the 'paramount' value in hacker culture is 'freedom': 'Freedom to create, freedom to appropriate whatever knowledge is available, and freedom to redistribute this knowledge under any form and channel chosen by the hacker' (Castells 2001: 46–7). Added to this are the values of spontaneous voluntary cooperation, anti-commercialism, and hostility to property and proprietary relations and institutional power.

The third layer of internet culture identified by Castells is virtual communitarian culture – arising from the online social formations established by early users of the internet, many of which were born of the countercultural movements and alternative lifestyles of the late 1960s. According to Castells, 'while the hacker culture provided the technological foundations of the Internet, the communitarian culture shaped its social forms, processes and uses' (Castells 2001: 53). Castells points out that while the diversity of virtual communities makes it difficult to specify a coherent and consistent set of values they all share, they do exhibit 'two major, common, cultural features'. The first is 'the value of horizontal free communication' – global free speech that circumvents the communicative dominance (and censorship) of media conglomerates and government bureaucracies. The second is the value of 'self-directed networking: the capacity for anyone to find his or her own destination on the net and, if not found, to create and post his or her own information, thus inducing a network'. This self-directed networking is a cultural 'tool for organization, collective action, and the construction of meaning' (Castells 2001: 54–5). The final layer of internet culture according to Castells is entrepreneurial culture – the culture of the business entrepreneurs and venture capitalists responsible for disseminating internet technology to society at large. Its cornerstone values are the high value placed on ideas, knowledge and innovation; the identification of making lots of money fast with freedom and success; the belief that the future is there to be made and taken right now. It is a culture of money and 'workaholism', a culture of 'superfluous consumption' aimed at 'immediate gratification' and withdrawal from social and civic engagement in favour of individual achievement and instrumental relationships. As Castells describes the denizens of this culture:

> they escape from society, as they thrive in technology, and worship money, with a decreasing feedback from the world as it is. After all, why pay attention to the world if they are re-making it in their own image? The Internet entrepreneurs are, at the same time, artists and prophets and greedy, as they hide their social autism behind their technological prowess. (Castells 2001: 60)

In Castells's formulation, these four cultures articulate to form internet culture: 'The culture of the Internet is a culture made up of a technocratic belief in the progress of humans through technology, enacted by communities of hackers thriving on free and open technological creativity, embedded in virtual networks aimed at reinventing society, and materialized by money-driven entrepreneurs into the workings of the new economy' (Castells 2001: 61).

Pippa Norris has a somewhat different interpretation of internet culture. She is interested to specify the *political culture* of internet users, by 'examining whether the predominant values, attitudes and beliefs found within the online world are distinctive from the broader political culture' (Norris 2001: 196). Of course, this implies a certain picture of 'the broader political culture' against which values of the internet population can be compared. For this, Norris defers to Ronald Inglehart's postmaterialism thesis – an influential account of trends in Western industrial political culture based on data from the World Values Survey (Inglehart 1997). As Norris explains, the postmaterialism thesis suggest that differences between the formative experiences of the generation that came of age in the early twentieth century and those of the baby boom generation of the later twentieth century have produced two distinct sets of cultural values among these groups. The formative experience of the generation of the early twentieth century can be characterized as one of sustained material insecurity, largely as a result of two world wars and the Great Depression and the absence of a fully developed welfare state. This generation's youthful experience of material insecurity gave rise to a particular set of cultural values. This 'materialist' culture 'prioritizes more traditional bread and butter issues such as basic economic growth, jobs, low inflation, and national security, the class politics of economic redistribution and the welfare state, as well as displaying more deferential attitudes toward bureaucratic and political authorities' (Norris 2001: 199). This generation also places high value on nationalism (over cosmopolitanism) and traditional, institutionalized, religious and moral authority. In other words, the culture of this generation is materialist in the sense that its primary concern is the achievement of material security in an insecure world, and support for the institutions that contribute to this security. In contrast, the formative experience of the postwar, baby boom generation is that of growing up in the midst of relative affluence and security. As such, the culture of this generation coheres less around basic issues of material security, and more around postmaterial values that take basic material security more or less for granted. This generation is more concerned with 'quality of life' and 'self-realization' than it is with basic material security. Thus, postmaterialist values include meaningful work (over basic job security); environmental protection (over economic growth); sexual equality (over traditional family roles); cosmopolitanism (over national identity); tolerance of diversity; secularism and free expression (over religious authority); and participatory democracy (over deference and bureaucracy).

According to this thesis, Western societies are at the tail-end of a generational shift from materialist to postmaterialist values and culture. Norris's hypothesis is that, given the demographic profile of internet users (affluent, educated and young), we might expect that the culture of internet users is particularly postmaterialist in its value/ideological structure. To test this, Norris examines data on the extent to which internet users exhibit sympathy with typical postmaterialist positions. She also looks at attitudes among internet users on economic freedom, understood as freedom from government regulation of the economy and from state intervention pursuant to wealth redistribution. (This set of economic/state values is ambiguously situated relative to postmaterialism – we might expect a postmaterialist to be opposed to government regulation that affects individual freedom but in favour of intervention that protects the environment, for example.)

In general, what Norris finds is that internet culture is indeed postmaterialist – probably more postmaterialist than the population at large – and that the most enthusiastic members of the online community are the most postmaterialist of all. Internet users are predominantly socially progressive, morally secular and economically neo-liberal in their orientations. Norris finds that American internet enthusiasts are, relative to the population at large, far more supportive of progressive social movements, less supportive of right-wing causes and more likely to self-identify as 'liberals'. She finds that cyberculture is even more secular than the culture at large: less inclined to fundamentalist Christianity; less inclined to assert the importance of prayer; more tolerant of alternative lifestyle and family relationships. Finally, Norris finds that internet users and enthusiasts are more likely to be in favour of business and the free market and opposed to government regulation, unions and the welfare state when it comes to the economy. Thus, she concludes:

> on balance, the evidence examined here suggests that the cyber-culture sympathizes with the values of openness, freedom and tolerance, on both the social and economic agenda, perhaps reflecting the broader ethos of individualism and alternative lifestyles that seems to flourish online . . . a culture that favors secular values on the traditional moral issues such as marriage and the family, sexual choice and fundamentalist Christian beliefs, as well as laissez-faire values with a minimal role of the state toward business and the economy. (Norris 2001: 210)

Norris also presents evidence that internet users in Europe exhibit a similar profile, ranking higher than non-users on most postmaterialist values, though European users tend to be less negatively disposed towards state regulation of the economy than their American counterparts.

Despite their use of differing conceptual languages, these two accounts of internet culture have many similarities – indeed, one might say that they are in agreement on positing a certain kind of freedom as the core cultural value of internet users – and they undoubtedly contain considerable truth. That being said, it is far from clear that specifying the culture of internet users should exhaust our consideration of the cultural implications of network technology. Network technology, in its various manifestations, infringes on culture in a variety of ways, and there are numerous possible ways of interpreting the cultural condition of the network society. For example, it is at least plausible to argue that digital technology is an instrument of the global homogenization of culture, the erosion of national and local cultural distinctions, the extension of American mass entertainment and consumer culture into every corner of life in every corner of the globe. As we have seen in previous chapters, digital communication technology is deeply implicated in economic and political globalization, and this extends to the cultural sphere as well. This is particularly evident in the role digital technology has played in the consolidation of massive transnational, multimedia conglomerates and the dynamics of neo-liberalism, which demand that national governments minimize their intervention in cultural industries. It is also evident in the technical difficulties of enforcing controls on transborder data flows in the network environment. Some celebrate the digitally mediated globalization of culture as a universalization of the values of freedom and democracy. Consider the following from Walter Wriston, one of the champions of the digital age:

> Modern communication technologies . . . are creating a global market that takes constant referenda on what in many ways is beginning to look like a global culture . . . All of a sudden, everyone has access to everything . . . Tens of millions of Chinese and Indians, Frenchmen and Malays are watching *Dallas* and the *Honeymooners* which, in their own way, may be more subversive of sovereign authority than CNN. The people plugged into the global conversation are voting – for Madonna and Benetton and Pepsi and Prince – but also for

democracy, free expression, free markets and free movement
of people and money. (Wriston 1992)

Of course, many experience the dynamics Wriston describes
as a cultural wasteland and a profound loss of autonomy.
It is hard to imagine how identity in the network society
could remain unaffected by a cultural condition such as
this.

Another, equally plausible set of arguments cuts somewhat
against the homogenization thesis, and suggests that the
primary cultural significance of network technologies is the
support they provide for cultural fragmentation. Most of
what was/is culturally significant about communication
media that preceded the internet derived from the fact that
they were mass media capable of constructing mass audiences
and mass consciousness. These mass media (newspapers,
Hollywood cinema, broadcast radio and television) gathered
the attention of massive numbers of people who all read,
viewed or heard the same thing, in the same form, from the
same central source, at roughly the same time. It was the
ability of these communication media to gather and construct
mass audiences that made them economically significant
as industries (because mass attention could be sold to advertisers); politically significant as tools of administration
and propaganda; and culturally significant as a source of
widely shared systems of meaning, symbolic interaction and
socialization.

Digital media are said to have technical characteristics
that, in one sense at least, undermine the mass media model.
The internet is certainly a mass medium in the sense that it
reaches increasingly massive populations. However, it does
not necessarily construct its users as a mass audience that
pays attention to the same things at the same time. As noted
above, the technical properties of the medium are such that
it enables a significant degree of customization or personalization of cultural consumption. There are a number of
reasons for this: the decentralization of production/distribu-
tion to the networked desktop personal computer has produced an explosion of highly varied cultural material
accessible from multiple decentralized sources; digitization of
material makes for ease of copying, alteration, appropriation

and distribution in ways unintended by the originator of the material; digital interfaces increase the role of individual preference signalling and choice making (and unpredictability) in the reception of cultural information; the asynchronic nature of the medium enables physically dispersed users to engage in cultural consumption at times of their own choosing; digitization has also enabled an overcoming of the 'bandwidth' limitations that previously kept the channels of cultural transmission to a relative minimum (the 500-channel TV universe; digital radio; the multiplication of news sources online, etc.), and so once again increased individual choice.

There are many possible interpretations of this dynamic of fragmentation. It is possible, for example, that claims about the demise of the mass audience under the auspices of the internet are greatly exaggerated. Global cultural and media giants have quickly gobbled up internet content and carriage enterprises because they understand that whatever threat the internet's technicality might pose to the reach of mass culture and the integrity of the mass audience, this threat signals a much greater opportunity to increase and diversify their hold on the cultural universe. And so critics of the fragmentation thesis argue that despite the technical potential of digital networks to diversify cultural production and consumption, the political economy of communication means that this medium is likely to become dominated by the very same interests and institutions that have historically controlled mass culture, and that most internet users, most of the time, will experience the internet as yet another medium of mass culture. At most, fragmentation means the reorganization of the mass audience into more precisely defined niche markets ripe for more customized marketing strategies.

Even among those who are more inclined to accept the fragmentation thesis, evaluations of its outcome are mixed. Some are pleased to witness the demise of mass culture: an artificial, industrial product that has robbed popular culture of its authenticity, diversity and dignity, and turned it into a commodity, or a propaganda device that generates meaningless spectacle, soul-destroying entertainment, false consciousness and political disempowerment. The internet, in this view, provides the means for an explosion of authentic, diverse, non-commodified cultural practices and forms. Evidence for this can be found in the many marginal or alternative cultural discourses that thrive on the internet, and in the communicative freedom and voice the medium provides to a panoply of subcultural forms and practices that were previously marginalized and silenced under the regime of centralized mass media.

On the other hand, many see in the technological fragmentation of culture the demise of the particular virtues of a common culture. The internet disintermediates culture, allowing a degree of customization and personalization that radically curtails our exposure to diverse cultural practices and artefacts, and undermines the common cultural experiences that might cultivate attention to widely shared common goods. In this view, the internet transforms the daily newspaper into the 'Daily Me': culture ceases to be an environment of traditions and practices we learn and share, and becomes simply a reiteration of our individual choices. It ceases to be something that joins us to many others in shared systems of meaning and instead separates us from others based on our unique combination of preferences, interests and choices. Thus, the internet, in this view, is the perfect instrument for the extension of a culture of radical individualism, narcissism and idiocy, a culture that presumes, ironically, that there is no such thing as culture – only self-determined individual choices, freely undertaken.

The opposition of cultural homogenization and fragmentation, and the varying evaluations of each of these poles, is but one of many similar oppositions that could fruitfully drive consideration of the culture of the network society. One could also examine questions about whether this culture is predominantly patriarchal or (as Castells argues) anti-patriarchal; as well as questions about whether the culture of the network society is one of politicization and civic engagement, or depoliticization and disengagement. There are many other variables that could be isolated for discussion. In all of these, there is also the persistent problem of trying to determine whether network technology has independent, measurable effects on the cultures into which it is insinuated, or whether the influence of these cultures themselves is the decisive factor in the elaboration of these technologies into social form. In short, the question of culture in the network society is very difficult to answer, especially at this early stage in its development, and all answers are compromised by our inability to stand outside these dynamics. Nevertheless, a full reckoning with the question of identity requires at least an attempt to reckon with the question of culture as well.

6
Conclusion

'In the midst of desire', writes Joseph Lockard, 'we sometimes function under the conceit that if we name an object after our desire, the object is what we name it' (Lockard 1997: 225). He refers here to the tendency to name online associations 'virtual communities', but the conceit he identifies just might pertain to the network society thesis as well. When we name a child, we choose a name into which we hope the child will grow and, somewhere along the way, it becomes impossible to imagine the child as having any other name. In the beginning, we hope the name becomes the child; in the end, the child *becomes* its name. Names do not just describe; they also prescribe. Another way to put this is to say that names have a *performative* aspect: they are not just labels; they also make things happen. It is important to consider the network society thesis – the proposition that networks have become the basic form and technology of human organization across a broad scope of social, political and economic life – in this light. In short, we must consider not only whether 'the network society' is a name that accurately describes the characteristics of contemporary society, but also the performative operation of this name as an active part, rather than just a neutral description, of the historical dynamics currently under way.

The first consideration invites us to evaluate how well the network model describes the society in which we live. Is it the case that the bulk of our most significant social, political and economic practices, relationships and institutions are best understood under the terms of the network model? Have these practices, relationships and institutions been reconstituted as flows between distributed networks of nodes connected by multiple, cross-cutting ties? Are networked information and communication technologies central to this reconstitution? Have these dynamics reached levels of extensivity and intensity such that we can identify them as the very core of a new type of society?

The safest answer to these questions is that it is simply too soon to tell. As the great modern philosopher G. W. F. Hegel wrote, 'The owl of Minerva spreads its wings only with the falling of the dusk' (Hegel 1952: 13). He meant to say that a historical change can only be expressed theoretically after the change has run its course, when its sun is setting rather than rising. By this measure, the network society thesis is neither right nor wrong, it is simply premature and, in any case, it is history and not us that will decide whether it is a name that sticks. This is surely true, but it still does not grant licence to dismiss prejudicially the possibility that we have something to learn about our current condition from the network society thesis.

To recall, Castells's theory of the network society identifies five attributes as definitive of the contemporary situation, each enabled by the proliferation of networked information and communication technologies:

- a shift in capitalist economies from an industrial to an informational base;
- the organization of capitalist economic activity globally, on the network model;
- reorientation of the temporal and spatial organization of human activity, in response to technologies that enable real-time communication across vast distances;
- distribution of power based on access to networks and control over flows;
- tension between localized human identity and placeless networks.

Are these attributes descriptive of what is happening around us? The material presented in the foregoing chapters would seem to suggest that, even if it is too early to name ours as the network society with any finality, this account does provide us with a viable descriptive language with which we might articulate a broad range of contemporary social, political and economic dynamics.

Digital technologies, at least in the affluent societies of the economically advantaged world, increasingly form the necessary infrastructure of everyday life. The central processes of capitalist economies (finance, production and consumption) have restructured on a global level to a significant degree, and these economies at least imagine themselves to be largely 'new' or predominantly 'knowledge-based'. Many enterprises have re-engineered themselves as networks and, for better or for worse, a great deal of work and employment has been reconfigured on the same model. The monopoly on political power once enjoyed by sovereign nation-states, while perhaps not entirely vanquished, has at least been significantly modified by nascent modes of global and domestic governance emerging on the network model. New social movements, organized on the network model and using network technologies, have become a significant political force both nationally and transnationally. Traditional political actors and institutions within liberal-capitalist states have also adapted to the spirit and utilities of networks, though not always in ways that are readily equated with democratic progress. Access to networks and power to determine what flows over them is a significant marker of systemic advantage and disadvantage domestically and globally. There also seems to be evidence that opposition to the globalization of economic and political networks dominated by Western/Northern capitalists has become an important source of political identity around the world. Finally, we have also seen that significant aspects of community and culture in the contemporary context can be effectively probed using the network model. Thus, it would seem that the network society thesis has considerable descriptive value, and so should not be set aside simply because of its excessive ambition.

Still, this ambition recommends moderation in endorsing the explanatory power of this theory. As suggested above, vocabularies such as that provided by the network society thesis do not only describe what is, they also establish expectations for what might, or should, be. The language of networks has worked its way decisively into contemporary discourse at both official and popular levels. Intellectuals, including Castells himself, have begun to refer to networks not simply as a sociological reality that we should recognize, but also as a 'superior organizational form' upon which an entire social order can, and probably should, be built (Castells 2001: 2). Here, the artifice of networks is naturalized and held up as a standard of near perfection. In the theory of the network society, networks are not just identified and described, they are reified and fetishized. In this respect, the discourse of the network society takes on ideological, as opposed to strictly sociological, proportions.

In his analysis of the rhetoric of the 'information society', Christopher May characterizes the ideological function of the name as follows:

> the arguments for the emergence of the information society have reinforced the dynamic they claim to observe by contributing to the reorganization of socio-economic relations they merely purport to 'recognize'. Postindustrial analyses which claim the information society is emerging have themselves contributed to the appearance of this new sociological 'reality'. By arguing that these changes are real and require a response, social and economic development has been pushed in a particular direction. (May 2002: 8)

Even a cursory reading of recent official and 'enlightened' popular discourse suggests that the rhetoric of the Network Society (capitalized here with intent) currently performs a similar ideological function. The 'Network Society' is not just a descriptive name. It is also an elaborate discourse that, in purporting simply to describe a set of contemporary social dynamics, provides a script that sets out roles, norms, expectations and the terms of dialogue. Thinking through the model of the network – nodes, ties, flows – certainly helps us to understand a great deal about, for example, the restructuring of capitalist enterprise and work, the disaggregation of state sovereignty, the rise and operation of new social movements, and emerging practices of community and identity formation. But when an idea such as this is elevated from heuristic device to the status of an all-encompassing social and historical fact, its function shifts significantly.

As an alleged fact, the Network Society becomes the standard for what is normal, desirable, and for what we can reasonably expect. At the present moment, firms are restructuring as deterritorialized networks, whose obligations to the places in which they are located, and to the natural and human resources they exploit, are dispersed to the vanishing point. In a Network Society, this is a normal and expected condition, legitimized by the terms in which that society imagines itself, rather than a situation open to fundamental criticism on the assumption that it could be organized differently. Workers are being reconfigured as flexible nodes in temporary networks, a situation experienced by most working people as a source of perpetual material insecurity. In a Network Society, this is an expected and normal situation to which we must adapt, rather than one against which we might express reasonable opposition. State sovereignty is being disaggregated into deterritorialized networks of shared power, and this constrains the possibilities of democratic representation, accountability, social security and the public regulation of powerful private economic actors. In a society whose norms are defined by the fact of networks, this does not pose radical problems for the legitimacy of authority, but rather simply establishes standards for what we might expect from the state in the network context. Human communities are organizing themselves on the model of networks, a model that may or may not provide for the sort of communal relationships human beings need to flourish. In a society where the network is understood as the natural model for all things, this is a question that is rarely even asked, because the organization of communities as networks simply reflects 'the ways things are'. At its most advanced level of articulation, the discourse of the Network Society not only normalizes present conditions, but also justifies political, social and economic measures that might otherwise be negotiable. At this point, to choose but one example, changes in labour law that support the casualization of the workforce can be uncritically justified *because we live in a Network Society*.

The distinction I am drawing here is between the network society thesis as a tool of investigation and interpretation, and the rhetoric of the Network Society as an ideological discourse that serves a performative, prescriptive function. What I have attempted to suggest here is that our appreciation of the utility of the former must be tempered by a recognition of the liabilities of the latter. Whether these two operations can be effectively separated is a difficult question to answer. Perhaps it is enough that we are aware of this problem. In any case, it will be history, and not us, that will ultimately decide whether those who spoke the language of the network society were actually on to something, or merely up to something.

References

Abbate, J. 2000. *Inventing the Internet*. Cambridge, MA: MIT Press.

Aglietta, M. 1979. *A Theory of Capitalist Regulation: The US Experience*. London: New Left Books.

Agre, P., and D. Schuler (eds) 1997. *Reinventing Technology, Rediscovering Community: Critical Exploration of Computing as a Social Practice*. Greenwood, CT: Ablex.

Amin, A. 1994. *Post-Fordism: A Reader*. Oxford: Blackwell.

Anderson, B. 1983. *Imagined Communities: Reflections on the Origins and Spread of Nationalism*. London: Verso.

Anderson, B., and K. Tracey 2002. Digital living: The impact (or otherwise) of the internet on everyday British life. In B. Wellman and C. Haythornethwaite (eds), *The Internet in Everyday Life*. London: Blackwell, 139–63.

Appadurai, A. 1996. *Modernity at Large: Cultural Dimensions of Globalization*. Minneapolis: University of Minnesota Press.

Archibugi, D., D. Held and M. Köhler 1998. *Re-imagining Political Community: Studies in Cosmopolitan Democracy*. Cambridge: Polity.

Bacon, F. 1900. *Advancement of Learning and Novum Organum*. London: Colonial Press.

Bailey, C. 2001. Virtual skin: articulating race in cyberspace. In D. Trend (ed.), *Reading Digital Culture*. Oxford: Blackwell.

Barney, D. 2000. *Prometheus Wired: The Hope for Democracy in the Age of Network Technology*. Chicago: University of Chicago Press.

Barney, D. 2003. Invasions of publicity: digital technology and the privatization of the public sphere. In Law Commission of Canada (ed.), *New Perspectives on the Public–Private Divide*. Vancouver: University of British Columbia Press.

Barney, D. 2004. The vanishing table, or, community in a world that is no world. In A. Feenberg and D. Barney (eds), *Community in the Digital Age: Philosophy and Practice*. Lanham, MD.: Rowman and Littlefield.

Baudrillard, J. 1983. *Simulations*. Translated by P. Foss, P. Patton and P. Betchman. New York: Semiotext(e).

Becker, T., and C. Slaton 2000. *The Future of Teledemocracy*. Westport, CT: Praeger.

Bell, D. 1973. *The Coming of Post-Industrial Society*. New York: Basic Books.

Bell, D. 1979. The social framework of the information society. In M. Dertouzos and J. Moses (eds), *The Computer Age: A Twenty Year View*. Cambridge, MA: MIT Press.

Bellah, R., W. Sullivan, A. Swidler and S. Tipton 1985. *Habits of the Heart: Individualism and Commitment in American Life*. Berkeley: University of California Press.

Beniger, J. 1986. *The Control Revolution: Technological and Economic Origins of the Information Society*. Cambridge, MA: Harvard University Press.

Beniger, J. 1987. Personalization of mass media and the growth of pseudo-community. *Communication Research*, 14 (3), 352–71.

Benner, C., and A. Dean 2000. Labour in the new economy: lessons from labour organizing in Silicon Valley. In F. Carré, M. Ferber, L. Golden and S. A. Herzenberg (eds), *Nonstandard Work: The Nature and Challenges of Changing Employment Arrangements*. Campaign, IL: Industrial Relations Research Association.

Best, S., and D. Kellner 1991. *Postmodern Theory: Critical Interrogations*. New York: Guilford Press.

Bimber, B. 1998. The internet and political transformation: populism, community and accelerated pluralism. *Polity*, 31 (1), 133–60.

Bimber, B. 2001. Information and political engagement in America: the search for effects of information technology at the individual level. *Political Research Quarterly*, 54 (1), 53–67.

Bolter, J. D. 1984. *Turing's Man: Western Culture in the Computer Age*. Chapel Hill: University of North Carolina Press.

Borgmann, A. 1984. *Technology and the Character of Contemporary Life*. Chicago: University of Chicago Press.

Brand, S. 1987. *The Media Lab: Inventing the Future at M. I. T.* New York: Penguin.

Bruckman, A. 1998. Finding one's own in cyberspace. In R. Holeton (ed.), *Composing Cyberspace: Identity, Community and Knowledge in the Electronic Age*. Boston: McGraw Hill.

Callinicos, A., J. Rees, C. Harman and M. Haynes 1994. *Marxism and the New Imperialism*. London: Bookmarks.

Carey, J. 1989. *Communication as Culture*. Boston: Unwin-Hyman.

Carnoy, M. 2000. *Sustaining the New Economy: Work, Family and Community in the Information Age*. Cambridge, MA: Harvard University Press.

Carty, K., W. Cross and L. Young 2000. *Rebuilding Canadian Party Politics*. Vancouver: University of British Columbia Press.

Castells, M. 1996. *The Rise of the Network Society*. Oxford: Blackwell.

Castells, M. 1997. *The Power of Identity*. Oxford: Blackwell.

Castells, M. 1998. *End of Millennium*. Oxford: Blackwell.

Castells, M. 2001. *The Internet Galaxy: Reflections on the Internet, Business and Society*. Oxford: Oxford University Press.

Chandler, A. 1977. *The Visible Hand: The Managerial Revolution in American Business*. Cambridge, MA: Belknap.

Cheah, P., and B. Robbins (eds) 1998. *Cosmopolitics: Thinking and Feeling beyond the Nation*. Minneapolis: University of Minnesota Press.

Chen, W., J. Boase and B. Wellman 2002. The global villagers: comparing internet users and uses around the world. In B. Wellman and C. Haythornethwaite (eds), *The Internet in Everyday Life*. London: Blackwell, 74–113.

Coate, J. 1997. Cyberspace innkeeping: building online community. In P. Agre and D. Schuler (eds), *Reinventing Technology, Rediscovering Community: Critical Exploration of Computing as a Social Practice*. Greenwich, CT: Ablex.

Cohen, S., and J. Zysman 1987. *Manufacturing Matters: The Myth of the Post-Industrial Economy*. New York: Basic Books.

Cohn, T. 2000. *Global Political Economy: Theory and Practice*. New York: Longman.

Coleman, S., J. Taylor and W. Van den Donk (eds) 1999. *Parliament in the Age of the Internet*. Oxford: Oxford University Press.

Compaine, B., and D. Gomery (eds) 2000. *Who Owns the Media? Competition and Concentration in the Mass Media Industry*. Mahwah, NJ: Lawrence Erlbaum.

Cox, R. 1987. *Production, Power and World Order: Social Forces in the Making of History*. New York: Columbia University Press.

Croteau, D., and W. Hoynes 2001. *The Business of Media*. Thousand Oaks, CA: Pine Forge Press.

Crow, B., and G. Longford 2000. Digital restructuring: gender, class and citizenship in the information society in Canada. *Citizenship Studies*, 4 (2), 207–30.

Dahlberg, L. 2001. The internet and democratic discourse: exploring the prospects of online deliberative forums extending the public sphere. *Information, Communication and Society*, 4 (4), 615–33.

Dalton, R., and M. Kuechler 1990. *Challenging the Political Order: New Social and Political Movements*. Cambridge: Polity.

Deibert, R. 1997. *Parchment, Printing and Hypermedia: Communication in World Order Transformation*. New York: Columbia University Press.

Deibert, R. 2002. Civil society activism on the world wide web: the case of the anti-MAI lobby. In D. R. Cameron and J. Gross Stein (eds), *Street Protests and Fantasy Parks: Globalization, Culture and the State*. Vancouver: University of British Columbia Press.

Derrida, J. 1974. *Of Grammatology*. Translated by G. C. Spivak. Baltimore: Johns Hopkins University Press.

Dewey, J. 1964. *Democracy and Education*. New York: Macmillan.

Doheny-Farina, S. 1996. *The Wired Neighbourhood*. New Haven: Yale University Press.

Dordoy, A., and M. Mellor 2001. Grassroots environmental movements: mobilization in an information age. In F. Webster (ed.), *Culture and Politics in the Information Age: A New Politics?* London: Routledge, 167–82.

Dreyfus, H. 2001. *On the Internet*. New York: Routledge.

Dyer-Witheford, N. 1999. *Cyber-Marx: Cycles and Circuits of Struggle in High-Technology Capitalism*. Urbana, IL: University of Illinois Press.

Edwards, M. 1994. *Printing, Propaganda and Martin Luther*. Los Angeles: University of California Press.

Eisenstein, E. 1983. *The Printing Revolution in Early Modern Europe*. Cambridge: Cambridge University Press.

Elkins, D. 1995. *Beyond Sovereignty: Territory and Political Economy in the Twenty-First Century*. Toronto: University of Toronto Press.

Ellul, J. 1964. *The Technological Society*. Translated by J. Wilkinson. New York: Vintage.

Febvre, L., and H.-J. Martin 1976. *The Coming of the Book: The Impact of Printing, 1450–1800*. Translated by D. Gerard. London: New Left Books.

Feenberg, A. 1999. *Questioning Technology*. London: Routledge.

Fernback, J. 1999. There is a there there: notes toward a definition of cybercommunity. In S. Jones (ed.), *Doing Internet Research:*

Critical Issues and Methods for Examining the Net. Thousand Oaks, CA: Sage.

Feyerabend, P. 1975. *Against Method*. London: New Left Books.

Fischer, C. 1982. *To Dwell among Friends: Personal Networks in Town and City*. Chicago: University of Chicago Press.

Fudge, J., E. Tucker and L. Vosko 2002. *The Legal Concept of Employment: Marginalizing Workers*. Ottawa: Law Commission of Canada.

Galston, W. 1999. (How) does the internet affect community? Some speculation in search of evidence. In E. C. Kamarck and J. S. Nye Jr (eds), *Democracy.com? Governance in a Networked World*. Hollis, NH: Hollis Publishing.

Gellner, E. 1983. *Nations and Nationalism*. Oxford: Blackwell.

Gellner, E. 1992. *Reason and Culture: The Historic Role of Rationality and Rationalism*. Oxford: Blackwell.

Gibson, R., and S. Ward 1998. U.K. political parties and the internet: 'politics as usual' in the new media? *Harvard International Journal of Press/Politics*, 3 (3), 14–38.

Giddens, A. 1991. *Modernity and Self-Identity: Self and Society in the Late Modern Age*. Cambridge: Polity.

Gillespie, A., and R. Richardson 2000. Teleworking and the city: myths of workplace transcendence and travel reduction. In J. Wheeler (ed.), *Cities in the Telecommunications Age: The Fracturing of Geographies*. London: Routledge. 228–48.

Gilpin, R. 1987. *The Political Economy of International Relations*. Princeton: Princeton University Press.

Gitlin, T. 1998. Public sphere or public sphericules? In T. Liebes and J. Curran (eds), *Media, Ritual and Identity*. London: Routledge.

Global Public Policy Network. Publications. www.globalpublicpolicy.net. Accessed 10 Oct. 2003.

Grant, G. 1959. *Philosophy and the Mass Age*. Toronto: Copp Clark.

Grant, G. 1969a. A conversation on technology and man. *Journal of Canadian Studies*, 4 (3), 3–6.

Grant, G. 1969b. *Technology and Empire*. Toronto: House of Anansi.

Grant, G. 1986. *Technology and Justice*. Toronto: House of Anansi.

Gurstein, P. 2001. *Wired to the World, Chained to the Home: Telework in Everyday Life*. Vancouver: University of British Columbia Press.

Habermas, J. 1989. *The Structural Transformation of the Public Sphere*. Translated by T. Burger. Cambridge, MA: MIT Press.

Hampton, K., and B. Wellman 2002. The not-so-global village of Netville. In B. Wellman and C. Haythornethwaite (eds), *The Internet in Everyday Life*. London: Blackwell, 345–71.

Handy, C. 1994. *The Empty Raincoat: Making Sense of the Future.* London: Hutchinson.

Hannigan, J. 2002. The global entertainment economy. In D. R. Cameron and J. Gross Stein (eds), *Street Protests and Fantasy Parks: Globalization, Culture and the State.* Vancouver: University of British Columbia Press.

Haraway, D. 1991. *Simians, Cyborgs and Women.* New York: Routledge.

Harding, S. 1991. *Whose Science? Whose Knowledge?* Ithaca: Cornell University Press.

Harvey, D. 1989. *The Condition of Postmodernity.* London: Blackwell.

Hayles, N. K. 1999. *How We Became Posthuman: Virtual Bodies in Cybernetics, Literature and Informatics.* Chicago: University of Chicago Press.

Hegel, G. W. F. 1952. *Philosophy of Right.* Oxford: Oxford University Press.

Heidegger, M. 1977. *The Question Concerning Technology and Other Essays.* New York: Harper and Row.

Held, D. 1995. *Democracy and the Global Order: From the Modern State to Cosmopolitan Governance.* Cambridge: Polity.

Held, D., and A. McGrew 2002. *Globalization/Anti-Globalization.* Cambridge: Polity.

Helliwell, R. 2002. *Globalization and Well-Being.* Vancouver: University of British Columbia Press.

Herman, E., and R. McChesney 1997. *Global Media: The New Missionaries of Global Capitalism.* London: Cassell.

Hills, J. 1998. U.S. Rules. OK? Telecommunication since the 1940s. In R. McChesney, E. M. Wood and J. B. Foster (eds), *Capitalism and the Information Age: The Political Economy of the Global Communication Revolution.* New York: Monthly Review Press.

Hirst, P. 1997. The global economy: myths and realities. *International Affairs*, 73 (3).

Hobbes, T. 1968. *Leviathan.* Edited by C. B. Macpherson. London: Penguin.

Hoogvelt, A. 1997. *Globalization and the Postcolonial World: The New Political Economy of Development.* London: Macmillan.

Howard, P. E. N., L. Rainie and S. Jones 2002. Days and nights on the internet. In B. Wellman and C. Haythornethwaite (eds), *The Internet in Everyday Life.* London: Blackwell, 45–73.

Hutchings, K., and R. Dannreuther 1999. *Cosmopolitan Citizenship.* London: Macmillan.

Inglehart, R. 1997. *Modernization and Post-modernization: Cultural, Economic and Political Change in 43 Societies.* Princeton: Princeton University Press.

Innis, H. 1950. *Empire and Communications*. Toronto: University of Toronto Press.

Innis, H. 1951. *The Bias of Communication*. Toronto: University of Toronto Press.

International Labour Organization 2001. *World Employment Report 2001: Life at Work in the Information Economy*. Geneva: International Labour Organization.

Johnson, L. 2003. *The Co-Workplace: Teleworking in the Neighbourhood*. Vancouver: University of British Columbia Press.

Jones, S. 1999. Understanding community in the information age. In P. Mayer (ed.), *Computer Media and Communication*. Oxford: Oxford University Press.

Kalathil, S., and T. Boas 2003. *Open Networks, Closed Regimes: The Impact of the Internet on Authoritarian Rule*. Washington, DC: Carnegie Endowment for International Peace.

Katz, J. E., and R. Rice 2002. Syntopia: access, civic involvement, and social interaction on the net. In B. Wellman and C. Haythornethwaite (eds), *The Internet in Everyday Life*. London: Blackwell, 114–38.

Klein, N. 2000. *No Logo: Taking Aim at the Brand Bullies*. Toronto: Vintage Canada.

Kolko, B., L. Nakamura and G. Rodman (eds) 2000. *Race in Cyberspace*. New York: Routledge.

Kraut, R., V. Lundmark, M. Patterson, S. Kiesler, T. Mukopadhyay and W. Scherlis 1998. Internet paradox: a social technology that reduces social involvement and psychological well-being? *American Psychologist*, 53, 1011–31.

Kuhn, T. 1962. *The Structure of Scientific Revolutions*. Chicago: University of Chicago Press.

Landes, D. 1969. *The Unbound Prometheus: Technological Change and Industrial Development in Western Europe from 1750 to the Present*. Cambridge: Cambridge University Press.

Leiss, W. 1989. The myth of the information society. In I. Angus and S. Jhally (eds), *Cultural Politics in Contemporary America*. New York: Routledge.

Leiss, W., S. Kline and S. Jhally 1990. *Social Communication in Advertising*, 2nd edn. Scarborough, Ontario: Nelson.

Lessig, L. 1999. *Code, and Other Laws of Cyberspace*. New York: Basic Books.

Lessig, L. 2001. *The Future of Ideas: The Fate of the Commons in a Connected World*. New York: Random House.

Lipietz, A. 1987. *Mirages and Miracles: The Crisis of Global Fordism*. London: Verso.

Lockard, J. 1997. Progressive politics, electronic individualism and the myth of virtual community. In D. Porter (ed.), *Internet Culture*. New York: Routledge.

Luke, T. W. 1998. The politics of digital inequality: access, capability and distribution in cyberspace. In C. Toulouse and T. Luke (eds), *The Politics of Cyberspace*. London: Routledge.

Lyon, D. 1988. *The Information Society: Issues and Illusions*. Cambridge: Polity.

Lyon, D. 1994. *Postmodernity*. Minneapolis: University of Minnesota Press.

Lyon, D. 2001. *Surveillance Society: Monitoring Everyday Life*. London: Open University Press.

Lyotard, J.-F. 1984. *The Postmodern Condition*. Minneapolis: University of Minnesota Press.

Marcuse, H. 1964. *One-Dimensional Man*. Boston: Beacon Press.

Margolis, M., and D. Resnick 2000. *Politics as Usual: The Cyberspace 'Revolution'*. Thousand Oaks, CA: Sage.

Marx, K., and F. Engels 1986. *Manifesto of the Communist Party*. Moscow: Progress.

Masuda, Y. 1981. *The Information Society as Post-Industrial Society*. Washington, DC: World Future Society.

May, C. 2002. *The Information Society: A Sceptical View*. Cambridge: Polity.

McCaughey, M., and M. Ayers 2003. *Cyberactivism: Online Activism in Theory and Practice*. London: Routledge.

McChesney, R. 1999. *Rich Media, Poor Democracy: Communication Politics in Dubious Times*. Urbana, IL: University of Illinois Press.

McChesney, R., E. M. Wood and J. B. Foster (eds) 1998. *Capitalism and the Information Age: The Political Economy of the Global Communication Revolution*. New York: Monthly Review Press.

McGrew, A. G., and P. Lewis (eds) 1992. *Global Politics: Globalization and the Nation-State*. Cambridge: Polity.

McLuhan, M. 1964. *Understanding Media: The Extensions of Man*. New York: Mentor.

Menzies, H. 1996. *Whose Brave New World? The Information Highway and the New Economy*. Toronto: Between the Lines.

Morton, D. 1999. Birth of the cyberqueer. In J. Wolmark (ed.), *Cybersexualities*. Edinburgh: Edinburgh University Press.

Mumford, L. 1964. Authoritarian and democratic technics. *Technology and Culture*, 5, 1–8.

Murdock, G., and P. Golding 2001. Digital possibilities, market realities: the contradictions of communications convergence. In

L. Panitch and C. Leys (eds), *A World of Contradictions: Socialist Register 2002*. London: Merlin, 111–29.

National Public Radio, Kaiser Family Foundation and Kennedy School of Government 2000. Survey shows widespread enthusiasm for high technology. *NPR Online Report*, 3.

Nie, N. H., and L. Erbring 2000. *Internet and Society: A Preliminary Report*. Stanford, CA: Stanford Institute for the Quantitative Study of Society.

Nie, N. H., D. S. Hillygus and L. Erbring 2002. Internet use, interpersonal relations and sociability. In B. Wellman and C. Haythornethwaite (eds), *The Internet in Everyday Life*. London: Blackwell, 215–43.

Nixon, P., and H. Johansson 1999. Transparency through technology: the internet and political parties. In B. Hague and B. Loader (eds), *Digital Democracy: Discourse and Decision-Making in the Information Age*. New York: Routledge.

Nora, S., and A. Minc 1981. *The Computerization of Society*. Cambridge, MA: MIT Press.

Norris, P. 2001. *Digital Divide: Civic Engagement, Information Poverty and the Internet Worldwide*. Cambridge: Cambridge University Press.

OECD (Organization for Economic Cooperation and Development) 1999. *Impact of the Emerging Information Society on the Policy Development Process and Democratic Quality*. Paris: OECD.

Ohmae, K. 1990. *The Borderless World: Power and Strategy in the Interlinked Economy*. New York: Harper Perennial.

Pauly, L. 1997. *Who Elected the Bankers?* Ithaca: Cornell University Press.

Pendakur, M., and R. Harris 2002. *Citizenship and Participation in the Information Age*. Aurora, Ontario: Garamond.

Pinch, T., and W. Bijker 1990. The social construction of facts and artifacts: or how the sociology of science and the sociology of technology might benefit each other. In W. Bijker, T. P. Hughes and T. Pinch (eds), *The Social Construction of Technological Systems: New Directions in the Sociology and History of Technology*. Cambridge, MA: MIT Press.

Piore, M. J., and C. Sabel 1984. *The Second Industrial Divide: Possibilities for Prosperity*. New York: Basic Books.

Plant, S. 1997. *Zeros and Ones: Digital Women + The New Technoculture*. New York: Doubleday.

Pollert, A. (ed.) 1991. *Farewell to Flexibility*. Oxford: Blackwell.

Porat, M. U. 1977. *The Information Economy: Definition and Measurement*. Vol. 1. Washington, DC: US Department of Commerce/Office of Telecommunications.

Poster, M. 2001. *What's the Matter with the Internet?* Minneapolis: University of Minnesota Press.

Potter, E. 2002. Anarchy makes a comeback. In S. Ferguson and L. Shade (eds), *Civic Discourse and Cultural Politics in Canada: A Cacophony of Voices*. Westport, CT: Ablex.

Putnam, R. 2000. *Bowling Alone: The Collapse and Revival of American Community*. New York: Simon and Schuster.

Quan Haase, A., B. Wellman, J. Witte and K. Hampton (2002). Capitalizing on the internet: social contact, civic engagement and sense of community. In B. Wellman and C. Haythornethwaite (eds). *The Internet in Everyday Life*. London: Blackwell, 291–324.

Raboy, M. 2002. Communication and globalization: a challenge for public policy. In D. R. Cameron and J. Gross Stein (eds), *Street Protests and Fantasy Parks: Globalization, Culture and the State*. Vancouver: University of British Columbia Press.

Reinecke, W. 1999. The other world wide web: global public policy networks. *Foreign Policy*, 117 (Winter), 44–57.

Rheingold, H. 1993. The *Virtual Community: Homesteading on the Electronic Frontier*. Reading, MS: Addison-Wesley.

Robins, K. 2000. Cyberspace and the world we live in. In D. Bell and B. Kennedy (eds), *The Cybercultures Reader*. London: Routledge.

Robins, K., and F. Webster 1988. Cybernetic capitalism: information, technology and everyday life. In V. Mosco and J. Wasko (eds), *The Political Economy of Information*. Madison: University of Wisconsin Press.

Robins K., and F. Webster 1999. *Times of the Technoculture: From the Information Society to the Virtual Life*. London: Routledge.

Rochlin, G. 1997. *Trapped in the Net: The Unanticipated Consequences of Computerization*. Princeton: Princeton University Press.

Rosenau, P. M. 1992. *Postmodernism and the Social Sciences*. Princeton: Princeton University Press.

Rotenberg, M. 2002. *The Privacy Law Sourcebook 2002*. Washington, DC: Electronic Privacy Information Center.

Ruggie, J. 1993. Territoriality and beyond: problematizing modernity in international relations. *International Organization*, 47 (Winter), 139–74.

Rugman, A. M. 2000. *The End of Globalization*. London: Random House.

Schiller, D. 1999. *Digital Capitalism: Networking the Global Market System*. Cambridge, MA: MIT Press.

Schiller, H. 1986. *Information and the Crisis Economy*. New York: Oxford University Press.

Schuler, D. 1996. *New Community Networks: Wired for Change.* New York: Addison-Wesley.

Shapiro, A. 1999. *The Control Revolution.* New York: Perseus Books.

Smith, C. 2000. British political parties. In J. Hoff, I. Horrocks and P. Tops (eds), *Democratic Governance and New Technology.* London: Routledge.

Smith, P., and E. Smythe 2001. Globalization, citizenship and technology: the Multilateral Agreement on Investment meets the internet. In F. Webster (ed.), *Culture and Politics in the Information Age: A New Politics?* London: Routledge.

Stone, A. R. 1992. Will the real body please stand up? Boundary stories about virtual cultures. In M. Benedikt (ed.), *Cyberspace: First Steps.* Cambridge, MA: MIT Press.

Strange, S. 1986. *Casino Capitalism.* Oxford: Blackwell.

Strange, S. 1998. *Mad Money.* Manchester: Manchester University Press.

Sunstein, C. 2001. *Republic.com.* Princeton: Princeton University Press.

Tarrow, S. 1998. *Power in Movement: Social Movements and Contentious Politics.* Cambridge: Cambridge University Press.

Thomas, T. 2003. Al Qaeda and the internet: the danger of 'cyberplanning'. *Parameters: U.S. Army War College Quarterly*, 33 (1), 112–23.

Tönnies F. 1964. *Community and Society: Gemeinschaft und Gesellschaft.* Translated by C. P. Loomis. East Lansing: Michigan State University Press.

Touraine, A. 1971. *The Post-Industrial Society; Tomorrow's Social History: Classes, Conflicts and Culture in the Programmed Society.* Translated by L. F. X. Mayhew. New York: Random House.

Traber, M. (ed.) 1986. *The Myth of the Information Revolution: Social and Ethical Implications of Communication Technology.* London: Sage.

Trend, D. (ed.) 2001. *Reading Digital Culture.* Oxford: Blackwell.

Tsagarousianou, R., D. Tambini and C. Bryan (eds) 1998. *Cyberdemocracy: Technology, Cities and Civic Networks.* London: Routledge.

Turkle, S. 1995. *Life on the Screen: Identity in the Age of the Internet.* New York: Simon and Schuster.

Turkle. S. 2001. Who am we? In D. Trend (ed.), *Reading Digital Culture.* Oxford: Blackwell.

United Kingdom. Secretary of State for Trade and Industry 1998a. *Our Competitive Future: Building the Knowledge Driven Economy.* London: Department of Trade and Industry.

United Kingdom. Secretary of State for Trade and Industry 1998b. *Our Competitive Future: Building the Knowledge Driven Economy*; *Analytical Paper*. London: Department of Trade and Industry.

United Nations Development Program 1997. *Human Development Report*. New York: United Nations Human Development Report Office.

United States Department of Commerce 2002. *A Nation Online: How Americans are Expanding Their Use of the Internet*. Washington, DC: US Department of Commerce.

Vaidhyanthan, S. 2001. *Copyrights and Copywrongs: The Rise of Intellectual Property and How it Threatens Creativity*. New York: New York University Press.

Vosko, L. 2000. *Temporary Work: The Gendered Rise of a Precarious Employment Relationship*. Toronto: University of Toronto Press.

Wakeford, N. 1997. Cyberqueer, In A. Medhurst and S. Munt (eds), *Lesbian and Gay Studies: A Critical Introduction*. London: Cassell.

Ward, S., and R. Gibson 1998. The first internet election? U. K. political parties and campaigning in cyberspace. In I. Crewe, B. Gosschalk and J. Bartle (eds), *Political Communications: Why Labour Won the General Election of 1997*. London: Frank Cass.

Webber, M. 1963. Order in diversity: community without propinquity. In L. Wingo Jr (ed.), *Cities and Space*. Baltimore: Johns Hopkins University Press.

Weber, M. 1958. *The Protestant Ethic and the Spirit of Capitalism*. Translated by Talcott Parsons. New York: Scribner's.

Webster, F. 2001. A new politics? In F. Webster (ed.), *Culture and Politics in the Information Age: A New Politics?* London: Routledge.

Weizenbaum, J. 1976. *Computer Power and Human Reason: From Judgment to Calculation*. San Francisco: W. H. Freeman.

Wellman, B. 1979. The community question. *American Journal of Sociology*, 84, 1201–31.

Wellman, B. 2001. Physical place and cyberplace: the rise of networked individualism. *International Journal of Urban and Regional Research*, 25, 227–52.

Wellman, B., and M. Gulia 1999. Virtual communities as communities: net surfers don't ride alone. In B. Wellman (ed.), *Networks in the Global Village: Life in Contemporary Communities*. Boulder: Westview.

Wellman, B., and C. Haythornethwaite (eds) 2002. *The Internet in Everyday Life*. London: Blackwell.

Whitaker, R. 1999. *The End of Privacy: How Total Surveillance is Becoming a Reality*. New York: New Press.

Wilbur, S. 1997. An archaeology of cyberspaces: virtuality, community, identity. In David Porter (ed.), *Internet Culture*. New York: Routledge.

Willson, M. 2000. Community in the abstract: a political and ethical dilemma? In D. Bell and B. Kennedy (eds), *The Cybercultures Reader*. London: Routledge.

Winner, L. 1986. *The Whale and the Reactor*. Chicago: University of Chicago Press.

Winner. L. 1995. Citizen virtues in a technological order. In A. Feenberg and A. Hannay (eds), *Technology and the Politics of Knowledge*. Bloomington: Indiana University Press.

Witte, J., W. Reinicke, and T. Benner 2002. Networked governance: developing a research agenda. Paper presented at the annual meetings of the International Studies Association, New Orleans, 24–7 March. Available online at www.isanet.org/noarchive/Reinicke-Benner-Witte%20ISA%202002.pdf. Accessed 12 Jan. 2004.

Woodland, R. J. (1995). Queer spaces, modem boys, and pagan statues: gay/lesbian identity and the construction of cyberspace. *Works and Days*, 13, 1–2.

Woodward, K. (ed.) 1980. *The Myths of Information: Technology and Post-Industrial Culture*. London: Routledge and Kegan Paul.

Wriston, W. 1992. *Twilight of Sovereignty: How the Information Revolution is Transforming our World*. New York: Scribner's.

Zuboff, S. 1988. *In the Age of the Smart Machine*. New York: Basic Books.

Index